Documentaries

a teacher's guide

revised edition

Jo Wilcock

Auteur

Jo Wilcock

is the former Director of Southern Film Education and has been teaching Film and
Media Studies for over 10 years. She is currently the Regional Manager: South East for
Skillset, the Sector Skills Council for the audiovisual industry.

Acknowledgements

Thanks to BFI Video Publishing for help with stills; *The Guardian* for permission to
reproduce 'The Iceman Cometh'; and Becky Parry at the Showroom Cinema, Sheffield,
for advice regarding DOC Fest. Thanks also to Paul Smith at Tartan Video.

Dedication

To G - for your enduring patience and support, and to wee J for lighting up my life.

First published 2000. Revised edition first published 2004.

by Auteur

The Old Surgery 9 Pulford Road, Leighton Buzzard, Bedfordshire LU7 1AB

© Auteur Publishing, 2000, 2004

ISBN 1 903663 00 8

Auteur on the internet: http://www.auteur.co.uk

Designed and typeset by Black Cat Studio, Spalding. This edition designed and typeset
by Loaf, Cottenham.

Printed by The Direct Printing Company, Brixworth, Northamptonshire.

Contents

'There's nothing like the camera for getting around ... it can see round corners ... upways, downways, all the way around. It can put a telescope at the end of a lens. It can ... look through a microscope ... it's capable of a variety of observations...'

John Grierson, in his last interview in 1972

Source: Kevin MacDonald and Mark Cousins, *Imagining Reality: The Faber Book of Documentary***, London: Faber, 1998, p96**

Introduction

General Introduction

This publication is aimed at teachers of **Media Studies** at **GCSE**, **GNVQ**, **BTEC**, and **A Level** and is written within a framework that adheres to the all-important four key concepts of Audience, Language, Institutions and Representation.

This **Teacher's Guide** covers the TV documentary genre in terms of discussing the current prevalence in television schedules of docusoaps, dramadocs and institutional documentaries. More widely, it provides a broader context for the study of documentary, looking at the history of the genre, key movements in that history (such as direct cinema and *cinéma-vérité*) and pioneering figures (Robert Flaherty, John Grierson and Nick Broomfield). In addition to the discussion of the theory associated with the genre there is information about the practical nature of the genre, developments in the technology and the conventions employed by practitioners.

Each topic area is discussed in an easy-to-understand way, the aim being to provide the teacher with a comprehensive unit of work while instilling confidence in the teacher when faced with delivering this topic in the classroom. Key areas are illustrated by case studies and key terms are explained via definitions and examples.

The **Teacher's Guide** stands as a unique classroom resource but has been written alongside the *Documentaries:* **Classroom Resources** pack. The **Classroom Resources** contains numerous suggested tasks (written and practical) that support the contents of this pack, as well as adhering to curriculum

Definition of 'documentary':

'The use of the film medium to interpret creatively and in social terms the life of the people as it exists in reality.'
Paul Rotha, 1939

requirements. In addition the activities pack contains a useful glossary of key terms associated with the documentary genre that, though intended for student use, will also be useful for teachers.

[Publisher's note: This **Teacher's Guide** has been revised and updated in 2004 to take account of two developments since the first edition appeared in 2000 – the phenomenal uptake across all channels of so-called 'reality TV' programming, and the increased profile of documentaries in cinemas. Two entirely new chapters have been added, and the text has been revised throughout.]

So What is a Documentary?

According to Jeremy Gibson, Head of Features at BBC Bristol, a good documentary should fulfil the following criteria:

> '... it ought to know what it's trying to find and really expose something ... if the documentary has the privilege of access to an institution or to a relationship, then it should be careful not to abuse the access, then the documentary can deliver something that's really important ... in other areas of documentary, you want something emotional to happen to you whilst watching ... there needs to be a point to it ... it should make a contribution that is worthwhile...'
> **Source: www.bbc.co.uk/education/archive/talent2000**

The documentary genre has had a rough ride in terms of its popularity. Until only recently people considered the genre to be dry and stuffy, dealing in topics that were too heavy and failed to compete with the escapism that narrative cinema offered. The idea of something factual seeking to educate can alienate an audience instead. Yet the fact remains that documentaries are capable of entertaining, persuading and provoking, something which a lot of mainstream cinema often fails to do!

Documentary is somewhat difficult to define as its meaning has changed over time, particularly with the development of technology (and you will find scattered throughout the text different definitions of what constitutes a documentary). Nevertheless, regardless of how sophisticated the technology available, documentary has as its central tenet the notion that it focuses on and questions actual people and events, often in a social context, thus placing the audience in a position to form an opinion about who or what we are seeing. In making some kind of social criticism the documentary may seek to persuade its audience of its argument. The documentary is a collaboration between the film-maker and his/her subject and it can be set in the present, reflect upon the past or may even consider the future.

Documentaries purport to present factual information about the world. We understand that what we are seeing is a documentary as it is often flagged as such via on-screen labels (e.g. a person's name and their job title, the time and the place where the action is taking place). This leads us to believe that the people, places and events that we are watching do actually exist and that the information conveyed to us is accurate. We, as the audience, are asked to trust the content and the film-maker's intentions.

In presenting information to us the documentary film-maker may use a number of devices. For example:

- s/he may record events as they actually occur;
- information may be presented using visual aids, such as charts and maps;
- some events may be staged for the camera.

It is also important to note that a documentary crew usually consists only of one camera operator and a sound person, so that they can remain mobile while filming.

On the whole a documentary makes a stand about something or someone, states an opinion and then advocates a solution or conclusion. The film will often use rhetoric to persuade an audience, but it uses facts to convey this line of argument. Persuasion is attempted using

Definition of 'documentary':

'... the creative use of actuality.'
John Grierson

Definition of 'documentary':

'I hate the word "documentary", I think it smells of dust and boredom. I think "Realist" films much the best.'

Alberto Cavalcanti

evidence, with the evidence presented as fact. It may be partisan and lacking in objectivity but it is still presented as trustworthy. Even an unreliable documentary is still a documentary (cf. section on mediation, in particular the case study on Michael Moore's *Roger and Me*, 1989).

Documentary Techniques

Generally speaking there are **three** types of documentary:

1) **Compilation film** - where the film comprises an assembly of archive images, such as newsreel footage.

2) **Interview (or 'talking heads')** - where testimonies are recorded about people, events or social movements.

3) **Direct cinema** - where an event is recorded 'as it happens' with minimal interference from the film-maker.

Often a single documentary will employ all of these forms - it may feature archival footage, interviews and fly-on-the wall shots. Additionally, documentaries may use animation to get their point across (e.g. an instructional film may demonstrate how a machine works or a war documentary may indicate troop movement in this way).

Documentaries often use a **narrative form** - in other words they tell us a story. Like fiction they also need good characters, tension and a point of view. All of these things can be achieved via a number of elements: it can be planned or improvised; it can have a voice-over; it can employ interviews or merely 'observe'; it can use found footage or music. But always it must be based upon evidence. Increasingly, modern documentaries are less scripted then their predecessors and appear more observational, resulting in the audience arguably being placed in the position of a voyeur.

The genre also uses **parallelism** (i.e. asking us to draw parallels between characters, settings and situations), prompting the audience to actively compare and contrast these elements to identify their similarities. In so doing the audience makes sense of the unfolding narrative.

Frequently a documentary will feature a **narrator**, a device that enables the audience to receive plot information. The most common is the **non-character narrator** (or 'voice of god') who remains an anonymous intermediary, purporting to tell the audience the story. Alternatively, a **character narrator** is used, where the person telling the audience the story is actually a character in the documentary itself. By privileging one viewpoint in this way, the documentary may either be articulating the views of its makers or prompting the audience to seriously question the character's views.

Many TV documentaries use an 'authoritative voice' with whom we are already familiar and whom we trust (e.g. John Nettles - *Airport*; Andrew Sachs - *Children's Hospital*; Ross Kemp - *Paddington Green*; Robert Lindsay - *Castaway 2000*). Listening to a voice that we recognise has the effect of making the audience trust the information being imparted. Conventionally, voice-overs tend to be male (in the tradition of film trailers and Pathé newsreels) but recent documentaries, particularly those aimed at a younger audience, have started to introduce the female voice-over (e.g. Lisa L'Anson with *Ibiza Uncovered*).

Some documentaries organise their content into categories and subcategories as a way of structuring the information that is being conveyed to the audience and this is known as **categorical form**. So, the film may be divided into sections with each section focusing on a different viewpoint. This method of filming can be repetitive so the film-maker must vary the content in order to maintain the audience's interest.

The source of the **lighting** in a documentary usually originates naturally from the environment being filmed. Unlike a feature film-maker who may use additional light to manipulate the image that the audience is presented with, the documentary film-maker will usually only use what light is actually available, or perhaps necessary (e.g. to light interviewees).

Definition of 'documentary':

'Documentary - the presentation of actual facts that makes them credible and telling to people at the same time.'
William Stoff

The most commonly used **camera** is the hand-held camera - eradicating the need for a tripod or a dolly. The operator does not necessarily want a smooth camera movement, shaky shots making the film appear more 'authentic' and 'real', so s/he uses his/her body as a support. (This type of camerawork became popular in the 1950s with the development of the *cinéma-vérité* style.) The hand-held camera shot creates a subjective point of view (a.k.a. 'fly-on-the-wall'), that aims at an intimacy between the audience and the film.

Editing is a vital component of any film but documentary films characteristically rely upon it. There are several types of edit available, each rendering a different response from an audience due to the effect it has on the image:

- **fade-out** - this is when an image gradually darkens into blackness;
- **fade-in** - this is the opposite of the above and so the image lightens from blackness;
- **dissolve** - this is when the end of a shot is briefly superimposed with the beginning of the next;
- **wipe** - this is when a shot is replaced by another, using a boundary line which moves across the screen.

The editing process is a vital component in the attempt to convey meaning to the audience who are not originally present - editing is a way of interpreting an event in a comprehensible form. During filming the director will seek to create a sense of truth through spontaneity, but it is during the editing process that the material has to be selected, ordered and placed into sequential form. In other words, 'mediated'. In fact, even during filming choices are made as to the type of lighting, the type of focus, the angle of the shot and whose point of view we are watching, all clues as to the intentions of the film-maker.

Another consequence of editing is that it creates film space or **spatial relations**. Moving from one shot to another, the audience relates this juxtaposition through similarity, difference or development and creates meaning (e.g. if we see one shot of a person running for a bus and then the next shot is of a bus stopping we assume that the two are connected - they have a spatial relation to one another). You can read more about editing in the section Technology Used in Documentary Production.

In most films there are two types of sound - **diegetic sound** (i.e. when the sound has a source within the film, such as dialogue, sounds from objects) or **non-diegetic sound** (i.e. when the sound stems from a source outside of the film, such as a soundtrack, a narrator or a sound effect). Documentaries rely heavily on non-diegetic sound to prompt the audience to respond in a certain way. For example, music is used to dramatic effect in the BBC's *Castaway 2000*, particularly to accompany the behaviour of Ray the castaway who, with the help of the tabloid press, left the island early. When Ray drank too much and became abusive to his fellow castaways, his actions were often accompanied by crescendoing music to create maximum tension.

Documentaries are a necessary social vehicle for informing pubic opinion and with the growth of video more and more people have access to the means of production and therefore to expressing their opinion. Traditionally the genre has been thought of as a male bastion, with few exceptions documentaries tended to be made by a male director and crew. More recently important documentary films have emerged from a broader cross-section of society with an increasing number of female directors having success, as well as lesbian and gay film-makers (e.g. *Before Stonewall: The Making of a Gay and Lesbian Community* 1984, Greta Schiller, John Scagliotti & Robert Rosenberg; *A Portion of a Lady* 2000, Marco Chiandetti) and black film-makers (e.g. *Eyes on the Prize* 1989, Henry Hampton). The documentary genre allows for the expression of a point of view as well as the illustration of the 'truth' in a way which is flexible yet understood by audiences who have become accustomed to the conventions of the genre.

'In the first place, truly great documentaries are analytical, in the sense that they present the corner of reality with which they deal not as a truth there to be observed, but as a social and historical reality which can only be understood

Definition of 'documentary':

'Thousands of bunglers have made the word [documentary] come to mean a deadly, routine, form of filmmaking, the kind an alienated consumer society might appear to deserve - the art of talking a great deal during a film, with a commentary imposed from the outside, in order to say nothing and to show nothing.'

Louis Marcorelles

in the context of the forces and actions that produced it. Secondly, they are engaged, in the sense that they lay claim to objectivity, but actively present a case through their structure and organisation of point of view.'
A. Britton,
'The Invisible Eye', *Sight and Sound,* **February 1992, p.29**

Technology Used in Documentary Production

'[Recent changes in technology has] enabled film-makers to be less intrusive. When I started there were always three of us In the room: cameraman, sound recordist and myself; so that naturally makes a difference...we used to shoot everything on film, which is very expensive as a medium (roughly £100 for 10 minutes of filming time)...It imposed discipline...we made sure something interesting was happening before we switched the camera on; but...it was much harder to be there all the time. Today, much of our work is shot by director/cameramen, who are able to be much lighter on their feet with digital video cameras, which means filming costs practically nothing.'
Stephen Lambert,
Head of Programming, RDF Media, *MediaMagazine,* **September 2003**

Cameras

There are three basic types of camera used in documentary film-making:

- film camera (35mm, 16mm, 8mm);
- analogue video camera (Betacam SP, U-Matic) - these became widely available in the 1970s but are increasingly obsolete;
- digital video camera (Mini DV, Digi-Beta, DVCAM) - these became widely available in 1995.

The advantages of the video camera

- ### Cost:
  the film camera retails from approximately £10,000; the analogue video camera from £8,000 and broadcast quality

digital video camera from just £2,000; - the average cost of 35mm film stock for a 90 minute documentary would be around £5,000 while the average cost of digital tape stock for a 90 minute documentary would be around £100; the film processing and lab fees for a 90 minute documentary would be around £5,000, while there would be no such fees for digital tape stock.

- film cameras can be heavy and clumsy to use;
- cheaper film cameras are noisy, causing sound problems;
- film stock needs to be kept at a certain temperature and requires 'warm-up' time, which is costly when 'time is money' on a production;
- digital cameras are lightweight and portable;
- 60 minute digital tapes are half the size of a pack of cards;
- digital cameras record CD quality sound directly in-synch with the picture, saving the need for post-synching the sound.

Editing

Non-linear editing has revolutionised the video and filmmaking industry in general as it gives the programme maker an enormous amount of flexibility. If a documentary is shot on video (analogue or digital) it can be fed into a computer system and edited completely within the computer. The programme can be stored on a computer and changes can be made to any segment of the programme at any stage of the post-production phase. The way that it works also means that there is no generation loss due to copying. The master edit can be of the same quality as the original footage, unlike traditional editing where there will always be at least one generation loss.

If the documentary is shot on film, it can still be edited in the same way. It requires the negative to be telecined to video, complete with the relevant frame information. This can then be fed into the computer and edited as above. Once the editing is completed, the computer compiles an EDL (Editing Decision List) with all of the relevant information. This can then be sent to a laboratory with the negatives to be developed and cut in the traditional

Definition of 'documentary':

'In and of itself, the documentary is no more realistic than the feature film.'

Alexander Kluge

way. One of the key benefits of this method is that the director and the editor can view a variety of shots and edits and see the results, without physically cutting the negatives (as was previously necessary when editing using the analogue or linear method).

The advantages of non-linear editing

- ## Cost:
- a traditional three machine linear system costs around £10,000, whereas a complete non-linear system capable of producing television quality pictures can be as little as £2,000.
- non-linear editing can be done on location or nearby;
- different edits can be produced and viewed without destroying any of the film/tape;
- backers or potential backers can be shown the edits at an early stage of the production at minimal expense;
- the mechanical restrictions of traditional editing are removed since video and audio material can be stored onto a hard drive as digital data and then manipulated an infinite number of times before committing the final copy to a tape.

Recent technological developments

Steadicam: developed in the 1970s, this is the trade name for a widely used device that balances hand-held cameras gyroscopically, allowing for greater flexibility and fluid movement that is usually used to provide point-of-view (P.O.V.) shots. (The corresponding device made by Panavision is known as the 'panaglide'.)

Video Assist: this is an adaptor with a video camera inside, which is fitted onto a film camera. When shooting, the video images are shot simultaneously with the film images and through the same lens, allowing the director to review the scenes as soon as they are completed.

D.A.T. (Digital Audio Tape): this enables crystal clear sound recording that can be synched to film or video.

DVD (Digital Versatile Disc): this consumer format utilises MPEG-2 compression to allow a large quantity of material to be contained in one disc. The discs offer a wide range of benefits including cinema style surround sound, perfect pause, no rewinding or fastforwarding, language selection, photo galleries and multiple camera angles. Many companies have used this new technology to add behind-the-scenes documentaries and interviews to films released on this format, as well as such material as alternative endings and trailers. The phenomenal success of DVD has meant that it has largely superseded VHS video as a home entertainment format.

Definition of 'documentary':

'... all non-narrative genres - the documentary, the technical film - have become marginal provinces, border regions so to speak ...'

Christian Metz

The issue of mediation

'Think about it, fiction films are trying to imitate reality, while documentaries are reality! Watching real people, dealing with real Issues can be much more Interesting than watching fiction.'
Helen Dugdale,
'Stranger Than Fiction', *MediaMagazine* **September 2003**

One area of debate regarding the documentary genre is that of mediation. To what extent is a documentary truthful? Have the events that we are being shown been manipulated? And are we, the audience, being manipulated, as a consequence?

It is certainly true that the film-maker controls where the camera is placed, what is in focus and how it is edited together. However, in general, the director does not write a script for the piece or direct the action if it is unfolding as it is being filmed. By definition, a documentary is a record of 'real' events, people, etc. Similarly, the director may have no control or influence over the setting or lighting.

Nevertheless, staging is sometimes necessary and legitimate if it enhances the value of the film and may convey more information to us. For example, in his Second World War film *Fires Were Started* (1943), Humphrey Jennings was unable to film during actual air raids, so he used bombed-out buildings and set them alight, to create the impression of a 'real' fire, then used a genuine fire patrol to extinguish the blaze. Clearly this was staged but it represents an event that did happen and the reconstruction was deemed an authentic depiction and not a work of fiction. Indeed, today we accept a 'reconstruction' as a true representation of an event.

Roger and Me (Michael Moore, 1989)

Now regarded as a landmark documentary, Moore's darkly ironic, scathingly funny and deeply subjective film focuses on the inhabitants of Flint, a small town in Michigan where Moore was born, and the impact of a spate of redundancies at the eleven General Motors plants during the 1980s.

In the film, the larger-than-life Moore tracks down and attempts to convince the Chairman of General Motors, Roger B. Smith, to visit Flint and witness the devastation wrought by the shutdown. Unfortunately, the closest Moore gets to Smith is GM's public relations representative who explains that the redundancies are regrettable but necessary. In response Moore uses juxtaposition to good effect, showing Smith reading from *A Christmas Carol* for a GM television link alongside images of deputies evicting a jobless worker and throwing his Christmas tree in the gutter. Smith here is used as a symbol of corporate indifference, or worse.

The film, which adopts the style of a revenge comedy, purports to show what happened to Flint between February 1987 and August 1989, when the factories closed. The events depicted - the Flint Pride parade; a visit by President Reagan who eats pizza with the unemployed but neglects to pay; the opening of a new hotel and 'Auto World', a new theme park - were all real events, but the documentary came under fire as critics questioned the order in which the events took place. All of the events shown actually took place prior to 1986 when the factories started to be closed and Moore was accused of contriving the chronology in order to make the government look inept.

However, despite such criticism and GM's attempts to discredit it, the film was a huge commercial success and received praise in the form of numerous film awards including: Best Documentary (National Board Review, New York Film Critics, Los Angeles Film Critics, National Society Film Critics); Best Film (Toronto Film Festival, Vancouver Film Festival, Chicago Film Festival); Audience Award (Berlin Film Festival).

Moore's other film credits include: *Blood in the Face* (1991); *Pets or Meat: The Return of Flint* (1992); *Cheatin' Hearts* (1993); *Canadian Bacon* (1995); *The Big One* (1998); *Bowling For Columbine* (2002)*; *Fahrenheit 9/11* (see pg. 90).

* *Bowling For Columbine* was Moore's most successful feature documentary prior to *Fahrenheit 9/11* - made for $2.7million, the film went on to break box office records, making $21.2 million in the USA alone and controversially winning the Best Documentary Feature Academy Award.

A Brief History of the Documentary Genre

'The films began with "actualities" , the record of
more or less formal current events.'
H. G. Wells, 1929
Source: Kevin Jackson, *The Language of Cinema*, London:
Carcanet, 1998, p. 11

The word 'documentary' stems from the word 'document', meaning *'something that furnishes evidence or information on any subject'* (OED) and has been in circulation in the English language since the early nineteenth century. In relation to the cinematic sense of the word (i.e. a non-fiction film), it seems to have been brought to England in February 1926 by Scotsman John Grierson in his review in the *New York Sun* of Flaherty's Moana (1926). The OED gives the earliest usage of the word as dating 1930 in Paul Rotha's *The Film Till Now: The Documentary or Interest Film, including the Scientific, Cultural and Sociological Film.*

The term derives from the French term 'documentaire', meaning 'travel film', but Grierson later defined it to mean, 'the creative treatment of actuality' (although this definition has been the topic of much debate, some critics believing that it is so broad as to be meaningless). Other definitions do exist. Many film theorists believe that a true documentary is a film that focuses on social ideas and values and should aim to bring about a change in social and economic conditions. Others see it as a form of artistic journalism that can cover a range of subjects (e.g. fact, education, recreation).

The documentary genre dates back to the early newsreels and indeed to early film history since many of the first films were short factual pieces that recorded everyday

Definition of 'documentary':
'The use of the film medium to interpret creatively and in social terms the life of the people as it exists in reality.'
Paul Rotha, 1939

Definition of 'documentary':

'... [a documentary must seek to] reveal not "the" truth about the world around us, but "a" truth which is original and provocative.'

Michael Jackson, former Chief Executive of C4 and former Controller of BBC2

occurrences. Some people argue that the Lumiére Brothers made the first non-fiction films (or 'actualities'). Films such as **Workers Leaving the Lumiére Factory** and **Arrival of a Train at Ciotat Station** made in 1895, recorded everyday events with a single static camera and amazed audiences, who were seeing moving pictures of real events for the first time.

By 1910 film-makers from several countries were producing factual films based on general or special interests. In Britain, these included titles such as **The Durbar of Delhi** (1911), a two-hour film about India that was filmed in Kinemacolour, and **Scott's Arctic Expedition** (1911) which was released in several segments between 1911 and 1913. In the U.S., D. W. Griffith oversaw the production of **The Life of Villa** (1914) a seven-reel film which combined newsreel clips with studio reproduction to tell the story of Pancho Villa's insurrection in Mexico. Later that year John Ernest and George M. Williamson made **Thirty Leagues Under The Sea**, a five-reel adventure that focused on underwater life. Films such as these introduced amazed audiences to different cultures and exotic locations that they would otherwise never have seen.

With the outbreak of war the documentary genre was used by film-makers as a vehicle for propaganda, to heighten national pride in the war effort. Wartime documentary extracts were also included in some factual film narratives; e.g. **Hearts of the World** (1918) by D. W. Griffith used sequences that had been shot on location in both England and France.

Creative documentary film-making didn't really take off until after the war and many would argue that the first example of a creative documentary was Robert Flaherty's **Nanook of the North** (1922), a powerful, anthropological account of the Eskimo way of life. It was this film which proved that dramatic content could be derived from the factual depiction of primitive life. (See the case study on p.33). The success of this exploration of life in a distant land led to the production of others such as **Moana** (1925) also by Flaherty as well as **Grass** (1925) and **Chang** (1927) by Ernest B. Schoedsack.

Developments in documentary film-making were also taking place in Europe. In Russia, Dziga Vertov (loosely translated as 'spinning top') developed an approach to film called 'Kino-Eye' which adhered to a theory that underlined his political and aesthetic beliefs. Vertov employed montage to achieve 'the purest possible essence of truth' in his Kino-Pravda (or Film Truth, a homage to Marxism) newsreel series and feature length films, notably *Anniversary of the Revolution* (1919); *Kino Eye - Life Caught Unawares* (1924); *Cinema Truth* (1925); *A Sixth of the World* (1926); *The Man With a Movie Camera* (1929); *Enthusiasm: Donbass Symphony* (1931) and *Three Songs of Lenin* (1934). Along with Mikhail Kaufman and Elisaveta Svilova, he formed a group called Kinoks ('Kino-oki' meaning 'cinema eyes') who believed that the camera acted as a tool, capable of recording the world without any kind of human intervention and that only non-fiction film was able to do this. They rejected bourgeois, staged cinema with its stars, props, plots and studio shooting, insisting that the cinema

Definition of 'documentary':

'... only the documentary can really capture the spontaneity and immediacy of real life.'

Nick Broomfield

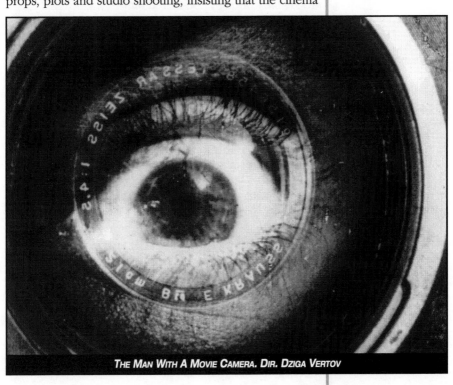

THE MAN WITH A MOVIE CAMERA. DIR. DZIGA VERTOV

Eisenstein's ideas on montage were based on D. W. Griffith's editing techniques. He saw montage as a vehicle for provoking an emotional response from his audience. He identified five types/levels of montage:

metric;

rhythmic;

tonal;

overtonal;

intellectual.

of the future was the cinema of fact. Vertov believed that the camera lens was capable of perfectly recording the world and organising visual chaos into a coherent, objective picture. His work aroused suspicion from Communist Party authorities who questioned his utopian philosophy and pioneering techniques. The public was also indifferent to his work, not able to grasp his use of slow and reverse motion, split screens, obscure angles and rapid montage, and Vertov acquired a reputation as an eccentric.

Other Russian film-makers who utilised the documentary format to great effect were Sergei Eisenstein in his film ***Ten Days That Shook The World*** (1928) which reconstructed events during the Russian revolution and Victor Turin's ***Turksib*** (1929) which followed the construction of the trans-Siberian railroad. These Soviet montage practitioners proved that it was possible to simultaneously manipulate emotion and disseminate propaganda through non-fiction film.

In France, a number of film-makers followed Flaherty's lead and made documentaries which focused on exotic lands: ***La Croisiere Noire*** (Leon Poirier, 1926); ***Voyage Au Congo*** (Marc Allegret, 1927) and ***Finnis Terrae*** (Jean Epstein, 1929). Elsewhere, Alberto Cavalcanti started the City Symphony documentary vogue - an impressionistic comment on life in the big city - in his study of Paris and its people, ***Rien Que Les Heures*** (1926). This was followed in Germany by Walter Ruttmann's ***Berlin - Symphony of a Big City*** (1927), a classic example of rhythmic documentary. Both films incorporated avant-garde and surrealist techniques, as well as footage of real locations to comment on the differences between the rich and poor. In Germany, the state-funded Universum Film Aktiengesellschaft (UFA) company established a special unit for the production of non-fiction films, under the orders of the German high command. The unit's aims were to boost Germany's image at home and abroad and promote Nazi ideology.

During the 1920s developments were also made in the field of the scientific and educational documentary. In America, Max Fleischer attempted to explore complex ideas in simple visual terms in **Einstein's Theory of Relativity** (1922) and in Russia, Pavlov's experiments with conditioned reflexes were illustrated in the feature-length documentary **Mechanics of the Brain** (1925).

Nevertheless, despite their advancement in artistry and technique, the screen documentaries of the 1920s lacked social relevance. This developed in the 1930s, in England, via the work of John Grierson (for his biography see p. 27). Working for the Empire Marketing Board (EMB), a British government agency set up to co-ordinate food supplies within the British Empire, Grierson proved that film was a powerful instrument of public education. Gathering a group of enthusiastic film-makers which included Edgar Anstey, Stuart Legg, Paul Rotha, Harry Watt and Basil Wright, he worked according to the basic premise that a documentary must be created in response to a social need and must fulfil a public service. Poetic in style and aesthetically pleasing, these documentaries were often reserved and underplayed, despite being motivated by a passion for social action, and served to prove that films about 'real life' were just as enthralling as any fictional drama.

Examples of documentaries made during this time include: **Drifters** (Grierson, 1929); **Industrial Britain** (Flaherty, 1932); **The Face of Britain** (Rotha, 1935); **Housing Problems** (Anstey & Elton, 1935); **Nutrition** (Watt, 1936); **Children at School** (Wright, 1937) and **North Sea** (Watt, 1939).

When the EMB was disbanded in 1933 the film unit was incorporated into the General Post Office, which was in turn taken over by the Ministry of Information when the Second World War broke out in September 1939. In April 1940 the unit was renamed the Crown Film Unit. Grierson moved to Canada in 1939 when he was appointed Film Commissioner and Chief Executive of the National Film Board, a newly formed organisation which was soon to be one of the world's most influential centres for documentary production.

The March of Time series.

Launched by Time Inc. in 1935, this highly regarded monthly series revolutionised existing notions of film journalism and succeeded in provoking a significant impact on the viewing public at home and abroad. Produced by Louis de Rochemont, the series based many of its ideas on the radio series of the same name as well as using the resources of Time magazine. With a duration of between fifteen and twenty-five minutes, each programme was comprised of a fusion of newsreel and documentary techniques, with many events portrayed through reenactment. Other style traits were pacy editing, forthright investigative reporting and narration that assumed an almost arrogant tone parodied by Orson Welles in Citizen Kane, 1941.

Meanwhile in the US, film-makers were equally motivated by social concern, despite lacking the central organisation of Britain or the institutional funding to guarantee a steady production flow. However, the films which American documentarists did make were frequently political and carried a blunt message (e.g. Iven's *The Spanish Earth*, 1937, called for greater support for the Republicans in the Spanish Civil War, with commentary and narration by Ernest Hemingway).

During the New Deal Era in the US, Government agencies did sponsor several social documentaries. For example, Pare Lorentz's *The Plow That Broke the Plain* (1936) dramatised the crisis in soil conservation in the Great Plains and the erosion in the Mississippi River basin was exposed in *The River* (1937). Between 1935 and 1951 *The March of Time* series was a key voice in America; combining newly shot newsreel material with stock footage and staged scenes, it covered a variety of

THE PLOW THAT BROKE THE PLAIN. DIR. PARE LORENTZ

factual topics with a conservative bias. The technical quality was high and its format was subsequently copied by many documentary film-makers. Conscience-raising editions included *Inside Nazi Germany* (1938); *The Ramparts We Watch* (1940) and *America Speaks Her Mind* (1941).

In 1938 Roosevelt established the US Film Service with Pare Lorentz as its Production Chief. Examples of their work include *The Fight for Life* (Lorentz, 1941) which focused on the problems of childbirth in the slums and *The Land* (Flaherty, 1942) a look at agriculture during the depression. However, the Film Service was disbanded in 1942 when Congress voted for its closure; many of the congressmen had felt alienated and pressured by the content of the documentaries. As a consequence, prior to America's involvement in the Second World War documentary filmmaking was achieved via independent means again. Notable examples of production are *Valley Town* (Van Dyke, 1949) a study of the consequences of automation on people; and *Forgotten Village* (Kline, 1941) an exposé of the conflict between tradition and modernity in an isolated Mexican village.

Prior to the war Germany had already been exploring the possibility of using the documentary genre as a vehicle for propaganda. In 1934 Leni Reifenstahl recorded the Nuremberg Rally, a massive Nazi party meeting, resulting in the extremely powerful *Triumph of the Will/Triumph des Willens* (1935). In 1936 she recorded the Berlin Olympics in *Olympia*, as a dedication to the supposed physical superiority of German athletes. Other politically motivated documentaries that were commissioned at this time include *Blutendes Deutschland* (1933), *Bilddokimente* (1935) and *Fur Uns* (1937).

At the opposite extreme politically, Russian documentaries were mostly made for local consumption by the political regime. Occasionally individuals made documentaries which advocated Socialism (e.g. Iven's *Song of Heroes*, 1932).

During the Second World War documentary production flourished since all of the nations involved in the conflict recognised its effectiveness as a vehicle for propaganda, military training and morale raising. The genre thrived not only in quantity but also in the technical quality of the production. Initially Germany was at an advantage since its propaganda machine had had much practice prior to the outbreak of war, under the guidance of Goebbels, Hitler's Propaganda Minister. In Great Britain, private industry joined forces with the government to harness the country's film-making talent to the war effort. The Ministry of Information took control of the Crown Film Unit and much of its initial output was designed to boost morale in the wake of the blitz. Later the films focused on information and instruction. Notable examples of British war documentaries are *Britain Can Take It* (Jennings & Watt, 1940), *Listen to Britain* (Jennings, 1941), *Fires Were Started* (Jennings, 1943) and *Western Approaches* (Jackson, 1944). At this time there was also a growth in fictionalised semi-documentary features such as: *The Lion Has Wings* (Powell, Hurst & Brunel, 1939); In Which We Serve (Coward & Lean, 1942) and *The Way Ahead* (Reed, 1944).

In America it wasn't until the bombing of Pearl Harbour that factual film-making was undertaken on any grand scale, largely under the control of the War Department and the civilian Office of War Information. Literally hundreds of documentaries were produced, ranging from orientation and training films for GIs to information and propaganda features. The American government also appropriated directors and other creative personnel from Hollywood (e.g. Frank Capra, John Ford, John Huston and William Wyler). One of the more celebrated outcomes of this allegiance was the seven films making up the *Why We Fight* series, produced by Capra for the War Department's Army Pictorial Service and designed to inform the American servicemen about the origins and causes of the conflict (some films of the series were also screened to civilians on the home front). Examples of the series include *Prelude to War* (Capra, 1943), *The Battle of Russia* (Litvak, 1943) and *War Comes to America* (Litvak, 1945).

Other war documentaries made in America at this time were **The Battle of Midway** (Ford, 1942); **The Battle of San Pietro** (Huston, 1945) and **The Memphis Belle** (Wyler, 1944). Walt Disney also contributed to the war effort by producing training and information videos as well as the feature length animation and live action colour film **Victory Through Air Power** (1943).

In Russia feature film directors were also recruited to produce war documentaries. **Fighting Film Album**, a series of reports from the front, were released every month from November 1941, soon after the Nazi invasion. Directors such as Gerasimov, Kozinstev, Yutkevich, Barnet and Trauberg were responsible for individual episodes. Many of the feature length documentaries were compilation films such as: **Defeat of the German Armies Near Moscow** (Varlamov & Kopalin, 1942); **Victory in the Ukraine** (Dovzhenko & Solntseva, 1945) and **Berlin** (Raizman & Svilova, 1945).

By the end of the Second World War documentary production levels took a drop, largely due to the lack of funding available. The only country to sustain its wartime activity levels was Canada, where Grierson had institutionalised the movement, and which continued to produce high-quality documentaries and scientific, instructional and experimental films for global distribution such as: **Corral** (1954), **City of Gold** (1956), **Universe** (1960) and **Warrendale** (1967). In Italy, documentary elements were used in several neo-realist feature films of the 40s and 50s, but there was little non-fiction production. After the liberation of France, documentary films such as **Le Retour** (Cartier-Bresson, 1946); **Night and Fog/Nuit et Brouillard** (Resnais, 1955) and **The Sorrow and the Pity/Le Chagrin et la Pitie** (Ophuls, 1970), harked back to memories of the war. Other French film-makers continued to develop their documentary techniques, while moving away from the painful memories of war, e.g. **Fabrebique** (Rouquier, 1946); **The Mystery of Picasso/Le Mystere Picasso** (Clouzot, 1956). Significant milestones include the science films of Painleve, the political films of Chris Marker as well as the

Key names in post-war European documentary film-making:

Belgium - Storck;

Holland - Haanstra, van der Heyde, van der Horst, Ferno;

West-Germany - Heinz;

Russia - Karmen, Kopalin and Raizman;

Bulgaria - Grigorov, Kovachev, Stroyanov and Toshava;

Czechoslovakia - Kadar and Klos;

East Germany - Bottcher, Gass, Heynowski, Schuermann and Thorndike;

Hungary - Gyaramathy, Szemes, Csoke, Kollanyi and Timar (the first two were prominent female directors);

Poland - Bossak, Hoffman, Jaworski, Karabasz, Lomnicki, Majewski and Slesicki;

Rumania - Boston, Nussbaum, Stiopul and Vitandis;

Yugoslavia - Babaja, Djordjevic and Skanata.

output of the *cinéma-vérité* movement under the leadership of Rouch in the 60s and 70s.

In the West the majority of productions were reliant on private sponsorship. By contrast Eastern Europe sustained a high level of activity due to government funds, and they were still supporting the production of films for propaganda purposes for the existing regime. In Russia many studios specialised in documentary film, resulting in the completion of approximately thirty to forty feature length documentaries and 1,000 factual short films each year.

With the end of government support Great Britain never quite regained its wartime momentum. Funding for documentaries came from private sources (mainly industry) with the consequence being that the films tended to be technical and scientific in theme. However, in the late 1940s there was a period of rebirth with the creation of the **Free Cinema movement** (a.k.a. 'British social realism'), under the leadership of Lindsay Anderson, Karl Reisz and Tony Richardson. The term grew out of the critical writings and documentaries of the three founders and the movement tended towards outspoken criticism of conventional class-bound British cinema and derided glossy, stylistic perfection. Calling for a break from Hollywood, exponents sought to film real people in real locations (in a similar way to cinéma-vérité later on) with a particular emphasis on the everyday working class. The Free Cinema movement rejected the idea that the documentary was a medium for mass communication and social improvement. Instead, the group used the documentary as a vehicle for expressing their opinions, with content taking precedence over style.

Fiction feature films made under the umbrella of the Free Cinema movement include:

Room at the Top *(Jack Clayton, 1959)*;

Look Back in Anger *(Tony Richardson, 1960)*;

Saturday Night, Sunday Morning *(Karl Reisz, 1960)*;

This Sporting Life *(Lindsay Anderson, 1963)*.

Each has an emphasis on working-class lifestyles and uses documentary techniques to underline a stylistic break with the British cinema that preceded them.

Key Figures of the Documentary Movement

John Grierson
1898-1972

No publication on documentary would be complete without mentioning John Grierson. He can be credited as being one of the leading figures in the history of documentary as a producer, director, theorist and driving force behind the development of the documentary movement in Great Britain, the US and Canada. It was Grierson who, in February 1926, first used the term documentary in his review of Robert Flaherty's **Moana** (1925) for the **New York Sun**, using the term as a derivation of the French word 'documentaire', meaning 'travel film'. At the time Grierson was interested in film from a sociological stance. He saw the genre on more politicised terms and was interested in the impact of the medium on the public, rather than from an aesthetic viewpoint, describing the documentary form as, 'the creative treatment of actuality'.

By 1927, Grierson had begun to research the possibility of developing a government-funded organisation for making education and propaganda films since he felt that the documentary form had the potential to serve the processes of democracy. In 1928 he established a film unit at the Empire Marketing Board and set about directing his first film **Drifters** (1929). The film, a documentary piece which portrayed a North Sea fisherman, was reviewed positively in Britain, which encouraged Grierson to expand the film unit further and take on a number of enthusiastic trainees.

While working for the government Grierson's mandate was '*Somehow we had to make peace exciting, if we were to prevent wars. Simple notion that it is - that has been my propaganda ever since - to make peace exciting.*' Grierson also adhered to Bertolt Brecht's statement that '*art is not a mirror held up to reality, but a hammer with which to shape it.*' And so it was that he chose to work with people who were socialists, committed to the notions of community and communal strength. (Source: Michael Rabiger, **Directing the Documentary**, 3rd edn., Boston: Focal Press, 1998, p.19.)

Grierson himself directed only one more film, **The Fishing Banks of Skye** (1934) as he decided to devote his time to developing the work of the unit as a whole and encouraging his group of trainees: Paul Rotha, Basil Wright, Stuart Legg, Henry Watt and Edgar Anstey. Indeed between 1930 and 1933 the unit produced one hundred documentaries, many of them with characteristic emphasis on social reform.

In 1933 the Empire Marketing Board was dissolved so Grierson moved the unit to the General Post Office (GPO). Here working conditions and finance were much improved, allowing the men the luxury of experimentation with form, technique and content, resulting in what is regarded as some of their best work (e.g. **Night Mail**, 1936).

During 1937, Grierson left the unit and set up the Film Centre, an advisory body which aimed to provide research information and production advice for documentary filmmakers. Between 1939 and 1945 he worked as the Film Commissioner for the Canadian Government, during which time he founded the National Film Board of Canada (a group still held in high regard today). However he resigned from that post and went to the U.S. to form The World Today Inc., a company which developed films to promote greater international understanding. By 1947, he had moved on again, this time to Unesco where he was the director of Mass Media and then in 1957 he returned to Great Britain to host a weekly TV show in Scotland, **This Wonderful World**, which featured a selection of documentaries from around the globe.

Grierson's filmography

Year	Title	Role
1929	Drifters	Producer; Director
1931	Industrial Britain	Producer
1931	Upstream	Producer
1934	So This is London	Producer
1935	Coalface	Producer
1935	The Fishing Banks of Skye	Producer; Director
1935	Ceylon	Producer
1936	Night Mail	Producer
1937	We Live in Two Worlds	Producer
1938	The Face of Scotland	Producer
1944	A Yank Comes Back	Producer
1952	The Brave Don't Cry	Producer
1954	Scotch on the Rocks	Producer

Robert J. Flaherty
1884-1951

'Sometimes you have to lie. One often has to distort a thing to catch its true spirit.'
Robert J. Flaherty,
Source: A. Calder-Marshall, *The Innocent Eye: The Life of Robert J. Flaherty*, New York: Harcourt Bruce Jovanovich, 1996, p. 97

Robert Joseph Flaherty became a documentarist after pursuing a career as a mineralogist and explorer. Indeed, his earlier career had an important effect on his film-making since many of the films focused on issues concerning the natural environment. His first film was shot in 1917 and was a study of the Belcher Islands. Unfortunately the majority (30,000 ft) of the footage was irreparably damaged by a fire, caused by a cigarette in his editing room in Toronto. Nevertheless, he made plans for his next film, a focus on Eskimo life, and received funding from the Revillon Fur Company. The resulting documentary **Nanook of the North** (1922) is an engaging chronicle of the daily life of an Eskimo family, which combines the editing style of fiction films with the real-life characters of the Inuit Eskimos with whom he had lived for years. The film became an international success, despite initial caution from the distributors about how the public would respond. It was also heralded as a landmark due to its use of elements usually employed in narrative film-making. The documentary was constructed around a linear storyline and many of the scenes concerning Eskimo life were 'staged' for the benefit of the camera. In addition, the film made excellent use of the camera to heighten the impact of on the audience, i.e. close-ups, tilts and pans.

The success of the film earned Flaherty the backing of Paramount Studios, enabling him to go on and make a documentary about the Polynesian people, **Moana** (1925). Flaherty was once more praised by the critics but unfortunately panned by anthropologists who felt he had opted for a romantic and vision of the Polynesians. Flaherty collaborated on two documentaries with W. S. Flaherty (**White Shadow in the South Seas**, 1928) and F.W. Murnau (**Tabu**, 1931), but withdrew from both projects before they were completed. He then moved to England in 1931, where he was associated with Grierson and the 'social documentary' movement of the 1930s.

It was while in England that he made his best-known British film **Man of Aran** (1934), a lyrical study of an Irish fisherman and his daily struggles. With this film (and others he made later in his life), Flaherty continued to receive a lot of criticism from colleagues such as Grierson and Rotha, since they considered Flaherty's work to be too concerned with poetic fantasy than with capturing the truth about the conditions of his subjects lives. This argument carries much weight when one discovers that for **Man of Aran** Flaherty actually constructed the family that is the focus of the film from a number of disparate residents of the island. Similarly, he omitted any reference to the huge house of the absent landlord, the man who was largely responsible for the islanders' poverty. These criticisms were explored in greater detail by George Stoney and Jim Brown's ***How the Myth Was Made*** (1978), a film that featured many of the surviving cast.

Despite being criticised for the romanticism of some of his work, Flaherty remains an indisputable force in the documentary genre, even being hailed as 'the father of documentary'. He recorded people's lives with his camera and then began to distil the meaning when he was editing Flaherty was a great storyteller and this was why he chose to adopt a poetic stance in much of his work; he made the simple and the everyday beautiful. His stories were a result of what he observed rather than a contrivance of what he wanted to see in a culture. He made his films for theatrical release and not for any specialised audience, approaching his subject with the heart of an explorer. Indeed, some have said that he was an explorer first and a film-maker second.

> 'All art is a kind of exploring ... to discover and reveal is the way every artist sets about his business.'
>
> *Frances Flaherty [Robert's wife] (Source: the BFI video of* Nanook of the North*)*

Flaherty's filmography

Year	Title	Role
1916	Untitled Film From the Far North	Director, Screenwriter, Producer
1922	Nanook of the North	Director, Screenwriter, Editor, Photography, Titles
1925	Moana	Director, Screenwriter, Editor, Photography, Titles
1925	The Pottery Maker	Producer, Director, Screenwriter, Editor, Photography
1927	The Twenty Four Dollar Island	Producer, Director Screenwriter, Editor, Photography
1928	White Shadows in the South Seas	Director, Screenwriter, Photography

1931	Country Comes to Town	Technical Adviser
1931	Industrial Britain	Director, Screenwriter, Photography
1931	Tabu	Director
1933	The English Potter	Director, Photography
1933	The Glassmakers of England	Director, Photography
1934	Man of Aran	Director, Screenwriter, Photography
1937	Elephant Boy	Director
1940	The Titan	Editor - English Language version
1942	It's All True	Story - 'Bonito the Bull' /'My Friend Bonito'
1942	The Land	Director, Screenwriter, Photography, Performer
1945	What's Happening Sugar?	Producer
1948	Louisiana Story	Producer, Director, Screenwriter
1949	Matthaus Passion	Editor - English Language version, Commentary, Performer
1950	Green Mountain Land	Producer
1951	An Investment in Human Welfare	Performer
1967	Studies for Louisiana Story	Director, Screenwriter, Photography

Nanook of the North (1922)

Nanook of the North is frequently cited as a seminal documentary text. Made between 1920 and 1921 and financed by Revillon Freres, this black-andwhite documentary was a pioneering feature length (fifty-five minutes) silent study of the Eskimo Nanook (who was then 40 years old) and his daily struggle to survive in an environment where nothing grows and he has to kill for food.

The Eskimos have few resources and no other race could survive the conditions that they view as normal, yet they are happy and it was this quality that Flaherty admired. The film is a homage to their struggle to exist; the soundtrack and language used for the intertitles reinforce this. Both the text and the music have poetic, melodramatic qualities that position the audience to totally empathise with Nanook's struggle. For example, when Nanook is out hunting an intertitle reads, 'Great hunter that he is Nanook saves the day' while the violins play tremulously, inviting us to hold our breath until we see that he has been successful in his mission. Similarly when the weather is particularly bad the intertitle reads, 'shrill piping of the wind, the rasp and hiss of the driving snow...', the language intended to heighten our sympathy for the family.

Clearly Flaherty was enamoured with Nanook and his people. There is no doubt that he developed a close relationship with Nanook and his family over the period of time that he spent with them on the island. He was making a record of a vanishing way of life and his subject was apparently all too willing to indulge Flaherty's preference for a romanticised 'truth' over actual everyday 'reality'. Flaherty dramatised events to get his feelings about the Eskimos across. Thus he films the men hunting with traditional harpoons rather than their normal guns and using archaic tools. Similarly, he staged parts of the Eskimos' 'daily routine' to suit the filming conditions, while other scenes were re-enacted to achieve greater 'authenticity'. When watching the film it is obvious that occasionally Nanook and his family are aware of, and act for, the camera (e.g. when the children have overindulged and are given castor oil as a remedy). This obviously influences the content and our reading of that content.

But overall the Eskimo appears natural in front of the camera, and, for Flaherty, this was perhaps the most important thing. We watch him as he

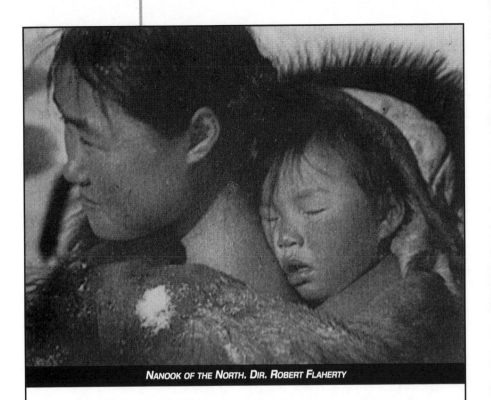

goes about his daily life: eating, sleeping, hunting and building a home and it all appears convincing. Indeed, the film appears to be 'in good faith', the apparent naturalism perhaps legitimising the film-maker's decision to stage certain scenes in pursuit of a 'truth' more universal than that of the Eskimos' everyday routine. Flaherty is at pains to open our minds to these people and employs certain devices to educate his audience; a map is inserted to highlight where Nanook lives in relation to the Western world and certain Eskimo terms (e.g. 'sentinel') are explained for us.

The filming wasn't without it's problems: a hand-cranked camera, insensitive film stock which required artificial light and poor weather meant that Flaherty had to employ special methods of filming at certain times. He took his camera, film and developing/printing equipment along with him on the journey so that he could see what he had achieved as he was filming.

A century of films

Derek Malcolm pick his 100 greatest movies. This week, number 63: Robert Flaherty's Nanook of the North

The iceman cometh

We have become so accustomed to television documentaries in which someone famous travels to a distant part of the world to view its inhabitants in their natural state that we have quite forgotten where it all originated. One of the fountainheads was Robert Flaherty, an American from Michigan who was as much the great Victorian romantic as any Englishman born in the late-19th century.

Flaherty was a pioneer of the documentary, and one of those whose work sparked many of the continuing arguments about truth and falsehood within the genre. His style is now often patronised as naïve and schematic. But if you look at Nanook of the North you can see where so much else has come from.

The filming of an Eskimo community took place over almost two years on the eastern shore of Hudson Bay, and Flaherty's goal was complete authenticity. He wielded his gyroscope camera himself, carrying into his harsh surroundings enough equipment to process and develop the film and show it to the Eskimos. Nanook and his family were real, but the film is not a straightforward recording of their everyday life: they amiably enacted some of it for Flaherty's cameras. But so honest and instinctive was their playing that it was undoubtedly truth of a sort.

The background comes to the fore, photographed in black and white with consummate dramatic skill. Though the film has no conventional plot, it tells a coherent story through its extraordinary images. It hints at that old cliche about the noble savage being pushed towards a civilisation that will destroy him. But it does so with a rare feeling for a timeless landscape and a way of life that had remained unchanged for centuries.

Caught on film... a pioneering moment from Nanook of the North

CREDITS
Director and photographer
Robert Flaherty.
US, 1922,
75 minutes

The building of the igloo is perhaps the most famous and fascinating episode. It is taken step by step, without the explanation that might render it more mundane today, though the way translucent blocks of ice are used as windows could hardly seem humdrum in any hands. But again Flaherty "cheated", since he had an igloo constructed to twice the normal size, with half of it cut away to provide more light for his camera.

When the film was released, it got rave reviews and no one called it a documentary. It simply seemed to be in a class by itself. It still is. Flaherty was never again to achieve such lack of self-consciousness and purity of style, though films like Moana, about the Samoan lifestyle, Man of Aran and Louisiana Story contained extraordinary sequences.

Flaherty had what was once called "an innocent eye", which tried to discover "the elemental truths that all men share". He was patrician, eccentric, obdurate and had the eye of a painter – the attributes of many good film-makers. He believed that if Eskimos could tame nature, then the rest of us could tame our more advanced civilisation. Perversely, Nanook of the North was made for a fur-trading firm. Perversely also, it was Nanook rather than the film-maker who became an instant celebrity.

Ironically, while Flaherty received acclaim for the film two years after it was made (disproving the distributors' initial scepticism), and people marvelled at how the Eskimo and his family coped in such adverse conditions, the 'star' of the film had died from starvation, while hunting in the Arctic. Nevertheless, in many countries the Eskimo's name lived on. Such was people's fascination with Nanook that in Malaya the word 'nanook' started to be used to mean 'strong man' and in Germany a dessert was manufactured and called 'Nanook', featuring Nanook's smiling face on the packaging.

Such is the intrinsic cultural value of **Nanook of the North**, and people's consequent continued interest in it, a soundtrack was added to it in 1939 and the print was recently restored to its full eighty-seven minutes.

Nick Broomfield
1948-present

'If Broomfield took up wedding photography, the divorce rate would be even higher.'
Film critic **Derek Malcolm,**
source: www.nickbroomfield.com

'Broomfield casually explodes that fragile construct of 'the objective' documentary in favour of a helpless absurdism totally in tune with the times. The tenets of an entire genre are implicitly mocked. He leaves in what others are trained to take out and doesn't appear to possess a traditional 'viewpoint' - which explains why he angers liberals and conservatives alike.'
Journalist **John Little,**
source: www.nickbroomfield.com

Born in London in 1948, Nick Broomfield studied Law and Politics at Essex University before graduating from the National Film School. His first documentary – **Who Cares** (1971) – was filmed across three months (and edited for eighteen months) using a borrowed camera and free 'short ends' of film; it was used by the Royal Commission as evidence on slum clearance and rehousing in Liverpool.

Twenty years later he is considered to be one of Britain's most successful contemporary documentary film-makers; a man who makes some very interesting choices where his subjects are concerned and a man who is something of a celebrity in his own right.

Citing Frederick Wiseman, Richard Leacock and D. A. Pennebaker as early influences, much of his work focuses on the bizarre and/or darker, more titillating side of life; people and places we are curious about. Broomfield's work is edgy, told from a subjective point of view; he is not afraid of making his own thoughts and feelings about his subject matter known and his point of view more often than not goes against the grain of accepted opinion. Broomfield doesn't seem to mind

'[Nick is] ... one of the few documentary film-makers in the world who actually manages to make money at it.'
John Powers, critic

treading on peoples toes or upsetting people in his quest for the truth; he strikes you as a kind of anti-hero figure hell-bent on uncovering the truth no matter who he has to upset to get there. He *appears* to be quite disorganised, almost haphazard in his approach to his subject but this is very much a deliberate device, employed to draw you (and his subject) into his work all the more. This is Broomfield's way of structuring the narrative to ensure that you stay watching to the end.

> 'The Selling of a Serial Killer *was a remarkable movie in the now celebrated Broomfield–Churchill style: loosely constructed in narrative terms, but tight in its polemics, featuring the languidly handsome and posh-voiced Broomfield extracting stunning admissions and awkward contradictions from his subjects and bamboozling them with his amiably dazed and boyish manner.'*
> **John Patterson,**
> 'The Ugly Chair', *The Guardian,* 23 January 2003

His work has attracted a younger audience who have previously seen the documentary genre as stuffy and dull. His provocative subjects have included the owner of an S&M parlour (*Fetishes*, 1996); a group of prostitutes in a brothel (*Chicken Ranch*, 1983) and women soldiers (*Soldier Girls*, 1981). The positions he takes in his film-making have been known to provoke controversy. One key example of this is *Kurt and Courtney* (1998). The film delves into the turbulent relationship between Kurt Cobain, the lead singer of cult band Nirvana, and his wife Courtney Love; a lot of the focus of the film is based upon Broomfield's belief in the idea that Love had something to do with Cobain's death (he commited suicide in 1994). Love did herself no favours when the scheduled screening of the film at the Sundance Film Festival was cancelled due to a court action from Love, who was ostensibly concerned with the copyright of two of Cobain's songs featured in the film. However, Love's motivation was widely believed to have more to do with the film's depiction of her, her relationship with her father (who blamed Love for Cobain's death) and the irony-laden scene where

Broomfield is manhandled from the platform of a meeting of the American Civil Liberties Union (who champion free speech) at which Love is being lauded and Broomfield is attempting to protest about her efforts to silence him. Of course the suggestion of a conspiracy together with all of this attention ensured that audiences were curious about the film and it was recently listed as seventh in the top ten grossing UK documentaries of all time, grossing $253, 997 (*Screen International*, 21 March 2003).

Broomfield's motives for making such controversial work stem from his desire to focus on topics that are edgy, since these are the stories that he believes will entertain an audience. Broomfield's work is distinctive in that the tone is often humorous and, furthermore, he does not set out to be objective. All of his films are extremely subjective (indeed some would say politically irresponsible) and we can see that what we are watching is his impression of people and/or events. In his (unauthorised) biography of Margaret Thatcher, **Tracking Down Maggie** (1994), the audience can quite clearly ascertain Broomfield's views on Thatcherism and its effects on Britain. (Interestingly one of Broomfield's sources of information for the documentary was a friend who worked in the Prime Minister's office and who gave him Mrs Thatcher's personal schedule, enabling him to follow her every move.) In the film Broomfield seems to almost intentionally fail to make contact with Thatcher herself, leaving him room to make his opinions clear and goad other key 'witnesses' to the Thatcher era.

Much of Broomfield's work is achieved by a small crew in one long take and is unscripted; the effect of the long take being the creation of a feeling of spontaneity. His fascination with his subjects is always apparent and his self-reflexive style means that he tends to intervene and question his subjects on the issues that he is curious about (moving starkly away from the tradition of the invisible documentarian, he has appeared in all of his own documentaries, often sound boom in hand, since the 1980s), as well as address the audience directly, sharing any difficulties he may be experiencing during the filming process. Indeed this self-reflexivity has become a trademark of his work – a visual signature if you will – and his work can be argued to highlight and question the film-making process itself. Broomfield's attitude to this is that someone is obviously making the film so why shouldn't the audience actually see the filmmaker at work. Oddly enough, in his most recent documentary, *Aileen: Life and Death of a Serial Killer* (2003) Broomfield has a very good reason to be seen in front of the camera; his first film about America's first female serial killer, *Aileen Wuornos: The Selling of a Serial Killer*, was used as evidence in Wuornos' appeal (later abandoned) and Broomfield was subpoenaed to appear as a witness.

> 'If you're making a film it's more honest to make your presence felt than to hang back furtively on the other side of the room, because no-one really benefits from that. That approach really is, to use the dread word, voyeuristic. You're there with all your equipment, but pretending you're not there...what's more important is the interaction between the film-maker and those being filmed, and that the audience is aware of that interaction so they cab make their own decisions..'
> **Nick Broomfield,**
> source www.screenonline.org.uk

So widely known have Broomfield and his film-making style become that he appeared in a recent series of TV adverts for Volkswagen Passat cars that parodied his technique.

> 'Big issues and strong stories are entertaining for viewers ... People who say that documentaries are not interesting on their own are wrong. [Documentaries are] ... as powerful as feature films with dramatic elements in them.'
> **Nick Broomfield,**
> source: http://www.tip.cz/internet

Broomfield met Joan Churchill whilst studying at the National Film and Television School and the pair have gone on to make several films together. Churchill had already become a renowned documentary film-maker in her own right (***Punishment Park***, 1971; ***Jimi Plays Berkeley***, 1971; ***The American Family***, 1973). Their collaborative work is arguably less confrontational than Broomfield's solo work. Their professional and personal relationship broke up in the mid-1980s, but they later resumed their working partnership.

> '*A precocious and influential film-maker, Broomfield is a documentary deviant whose style provokes his audience and often makes a mockery of his subjects.*'
> **Helen Dugdale,**
> 'Stranger Than Fiction', *MediaMagazine*, September 2003

AILEEN WUORNOS: THE SELLING OF A SERIAL KILLER. DIR. NICK BROOMFIELD

Broomfield's Filmography

Year	Title	Role
1971	Who Cares?	Director, Cinematography, Editor, Script

– made whilst at Essex University (funded by the BFI), focuses on a close-knit community in Liverpool.

Year	Title	Role
1972	An Eye for the Country	Sound

– reflections on the Lincolnshire countryside seen through the eyes of a schoolgirl and a farmer.

Year	Title	Role
1973	Proud to be British	Director

– made whilst at the National Film and Television School, a town's residents discuss what their nationality means to them.

Year	Title	Role
1974	Behind the Rent Strike	Director, Editor, Cinematography

– winner of the Grierson Award, this featured some of the subjects from Who Cares and focused on life in a lower-class housing project.

Year	Title	Role
1975	Whittingham	Director

– a focus on a mental hospital in Preston (for Granada).

Year	Title	Role
1975	Juvenile Liaison Part 1* (*'The film the police arrested'*)	Director, Producer, Editor

– funded by the BFI and used as part of a government study, this is a portrait of two Lancashire child-services officers and their 'relationship' with young offenders in the area. The BFI came under pressure by the police to withdraw the film from distribution and it was subsequently banned by the BBC but shown 15 years later in 1990 with *Juvenile Liaison Part 2*, an update on the young people concerned.

Year	Title	Role
1975	Trip Round Jenny (Dir. Dina Hecht)	Cinematographer

– a portrait of a prostitute in discussion with students and colleagues.

Year	Title	Role
1976	Fort Augustus	Director

– a portrait of a monastery.

Year	Title	Role
1977	Marriage Guidance	Director

– an exploration of relationships.

Year	Title	Role
1978	Tattooed Tears*	Director

– life at a correctional facility for young men in California

Year	Title	Role
1980	No Nukes (Dir. Daniel Goldberg)	Sound Recordist

– fundraising live concert with Bruce Springsteen, James Brown, et al.

| 1980 | Soldier Girls* | Director, Editor, Sound Recording |

– focus on women's basic training in Fort Georgia (winner of the Flaherty Documentary Award).

| 1982 | Chicken Ranch | Director, Producer (collaboration with Sandi Sissel) |

– focus on life in a brothel in Nevada (winner of the Grand Jury prize for Best Documentary at Sundance Festival, 1984).

| 1983 | The Making of Piscator | Sound Recordist |

– the development of a sculpture by Eduardo Paolozzi.

| 1986 | Lily Tomlin: The Film Behind the Show* | Director, Editor |

– portrait of the actress / comedienne and her methods of working (a court case ensued).

| 1988 | Driving Me Crazy | Director, Sound Recordist |

– a study of the making of a black stage musical, this film is arguably the documentary to have kick-started Broomfield's now trademark upfront film-making style.

| 1988 | Comic Book Confidential* (Dir. Ron Mann), | Sound Recordist |

– a survey of the artistic history of the comic book.

| 1989 | Dark Obsession (a.k.a. Diamond Skulls) | Director, original idea |

– Broomfield's only fiction feature to date, based on the story of the disappearance of Lord Lucan (nominated for the International Fantasy Film Award).

| 1991 | The Leader, His Driver and the Driver's Wife | Director, Producer |

– portrait of Eugene Terreblanche, South African neo-Nazi leader / demagogue.

| 1992 Monster in a Box | | Director |

– film of Spalding Gray's monologue.

| 1992 | Aileen Wuornos: The Selling of a Serial Killer | Director, Producer, Writer |

– unveiling the efforts to market Wournos's story to Hollywood and the ensuing media coverage surrounding 'America's first female serial killer' (winner of the BFI's award for Best Documentary).

| 1992 | Too White For Me | Director, Producer |

(collaboration with Riete Oord and Barry Ackroyd)
– portrait of Chicco Twala, born and raised in Soweto, pioneer of a new music genre called 'Township Bubblegum'.

1992	Bosnia Part 1 and 2	Executive Producer

– an account of the lives of a small Muslim community in Bosnia and the results of an ethnic cleansing operation by Serbian troops.

1994	Tracking Down Maggie	Director, Producer

– a study of the 'Iron Lady' after stepping down from the leadership of the Conservative Party.

1995	Heidi Fleiss: Hollywood Madam	Director, Producer

– portrait of a leading Hollywood prostitute.

1996	Fetishes: Mistresses and Domination at Pandora's Box	Director, Editor, Writer, Producer

– portrait of some of the clientele of a New York S&M parlour (garnered controversy when it was screened at the Edinburgh Film Festival).

1998	Kurt and Courtney*	Director, Producer, Sound

– a consideration of the circumstances surrounding Kurt Cobain's death.

2002	Biggie and Tupac*	Director, Producer

– an investigation into the deaths of two of rap's biggest stars (nominated for a Golden Satellite award).

2003	Aileen: Life and Death of a Serial Killer*	Director

– Broomfield is subpoenaed to Wournos's last appeal prior to her execution ('the most personal and most disturbing film I have ever made' won the Amnesty International DOEN award).

* Denotes collaborations with Joan Churchill

Documentary Styles

Direct Cinema

'I don't see how a film can be anything but subjective.'
Fred Wisemann,
Source: Nelmes (ed.), *An Introduction to Film Studies*, London:
Routledge, 1996, p. 186

The term 'direct cinema' was coined by American director
Albert Maysles, to describe the style of documentary that he
and his contemporaries were making in the 1960s as a result
of a lightweight, portable 16mm camera and highquality
lightweight audio recorders becoming available. The
introduction of these, together with film-stock which was
sensitive enough to give a good quality close-up
monochrome picture under most lighting conditions
(including hand-held lights) led to a revolution in
documentary film-making, allowing film crews to be much
more flexible. Gone were the days of bulky, virtually
immobile 35mm cameras; now manufacturers improved
their 16mm stock and accepted it as a professional format.

In 1959 a group comprising graduates from Drew
Associates, a company formed by Robert Drew (an
exjournalist) and Richard Leacock, joined forces. Their ethos
was to record events as they happened, without interfering
and in an attempt to transfer the style of photojournalism
to their film-making. The group - comprising Pennebaker,
Leacock and Maysles - was a key feature of American direct
cinema throughout the 1960s and the 1970s. Together with
Drew they made a total of nineteen pioneering films for
television, beginning in 1960 with ***Primary***. In this
documentary, for the first time, the audience were able to
follow a person (in this case presidential hopefuls John F.
Kennedy and Hubert Humphrey) moving from a car,

**The benefits of
16mm cameras:**

- *the cameras were
much smaller and
more manageable
than previously;*

- *the increased
speed of the film
stock meant that less
light was necessary
in order to gain a
quality image;*

- *consequently film
lights could be
dispensed with and
natural light taken
advantage of;*

- *all of these
conditions meant
that freedom and
spontaneity were
achievable for the
first time.*

Sound development:

• *a portable sound recorder, the Swiss 'Nagra' was introduced which was mobile and unobtrusive (prior to this sound equipment had been so large and cumbersome that subjects had to be taken to it);*

• *the invention of a portable recorder meant that filmmakers were no longer reliant on recording sound and vision simultaneously.*

The rules of direct cinema:

• *documentaries were not to include interviews;*

• *there were to be no rehearsals prior to filming;*

• *there were to be no staged events or commentary;*

• *no film lights were allowed;*

• *no dissolve edits were to be used.*

through a corridor, into a hall where he is about to give a speech and all in one shot! Drew saw direct cinema as a 'theatre without actors' and so the group concentrated on subjects who were so absorbed by their work that they almost forgot the camera.

In a similar vein to the recent Dogme '95 manifesto (written by Danish film-makers Lars von Triers and Thomas Vinterberg and to which the films *Festen*, 1998, and *The Idiots*, 1999, subscribe), direct cinema had a set of ground rules to which the members adhered (see sidebar).

The group's aim was a sense of objectivity, whereby the targeted events and people could speak for themselves without the conventional need for a voice-over. Ideal subjects for documentaries according to the direct cinema ethos were:

1) a person who is interesting;
2) a person who is in an interesting situation which s/he cares deeply about;
3) a subject where a conclusion can be arrived at in a limited time; and
4) a subject where there is easy access to events.

The group believed that the cameraman, the director and the sound recordist were all equal in status and were all film-makers, playing a role in an integrated process. They felt that the film-maker's relationship with the subject was personal and one of equality, and that an audience was active in its engagement with the film. Direct cinema practitioners wished the audience to be presented with sufficient evidence to enable them to make up their own minds and not be mere passive observers.

> '... the degree to which the camera changes the situation is mostly due to the nature of the person filming it ...'
> **Richard Leacock,**
> Source: Kevin MacDonald and Mark Cousins, *Imagining Reality: The Faber Book of Documentary*, London: Faber, 1998, p. 256

Direct cinema was conceived with TV in mind. In the 60s TV had poor picture quality, the black-and-white image being frequently fuzzy with viewers reliant on good quality sound. Image quality such as this fitted in perfectly with direct cinema's stance on camera framing and editing; anything more complex than jerky hand-held camera shots would have been futile for the intended medium.

The group's techniques have been increasingly employed by current affairs programmes such as **World in Action** and more recently institutional documentaries such as **Jimmy's**, as well as the **Video Nation** series. Interestingly, however, Roger Graef, a 'fly-on-the-wall' film-maker has commented that he found the BBC to be institutionally opposed to the ethos of direct cinema. Graef claims that according to the BBC, a documentary should be made by the following method,

> '... do a few days research and then restage what is "typical". Such a process involved the invasion by crew technicians moving the furniture and turning each location into a film studio.'
> **Roger Graef,**
> Source: Gill Branston and Roy Stafford, *The Media Student's Book*, London: Routledge, 1996, p.165

Few of the original direct cinema practitioners are still working today (except D. A. Pennebaker and Frederick Wiseman). Some of the documentary film-makers influenced by the movement are: Jan Troell of Sweden, Bert Haanstra of Holland, Kon Ichikawa of Japan and Louis Malle of France. But over time film-makers have found the rules too restricting and, it would seem, unrealistic to expect people to adhere to them.

> 'We were in fact, developing a new grammar which was entirely different from that of silent film-making and of fiction film-making. We were acutely aware that by this emphasis on sound we might be losing the visual basis for our medium. Looking back at the results it is apparent to me that the visual strength remained largely because of the avoidance of the interview, which I still regard as the death knell of cinematic story-telling.'

It was Leacock, who after experiencing frustration at his inability to move the camera while shooting sound sequences for Flaherty's The Louisiana Story (1948) decided, with a few others to adapt Walter Bach's Auricon camera (a 16mm camera with a built-in optical sound system, allowing the sound and the image to be recorded on the same film stock). They recast the body of the camera in a lighter metal to make it more portable.

'Obviously we have our own bias and selection ... we're not presenting the whole Truth ... we're presenting the filmmaker's perception of an aspect of what happened ... but within this, we're still trying to present the sense of what happened, what it was like to be there ... you make up your own mind ... we get extremely varied reactions ...'

Richard Leacock
Source: Kevin MacDonald and Mark Cousins, Imagining Reality: The Faber Book of Documentary, London: Faber, 1998, p.257)

Richard Leacock,
Source: Kevin MacDonald and Mark Cousins, Imagining Reality: The Faber Book of Documentary, London: Faber, 1998, p. 254

D. A. Pennebaker's interest in popular culture was seen in his now famous 'rockumentaries' **Don't Look Back** (1968, a study of Bob Dylan on tour in Britain) and **Monterey Pop** (1968, a look at the music festival which featured stars such as Jimi Hendrix, The Who and Simon and Garfunkel). **The War Room** (1993) was an account of the campaign to put Bill Clinton in the White House.

Frederick Wiseman focused on American institutions in his work: **Titicut Follies** (1967, a study on the criminally insane); **Basic Training** (1971, a study of the American Army); **Central Park** (1989); **Hospital** (1970); **Meat** (1976); **The Store** (1983) and **Missile** (1988).

Albert and David Maysles made many films about the famous including: **The Beatles in the USA** (1964); **Meet Marlon Brando** (1965); **Gimme Shelter** (1970, about the infamous Rolling Stones concert in Altamont); **Mohammed and Larry** (1980, about the boxers Mohammed Ali and Larry Holmes); and the not so famous **Salesmen** (1969, a focus on four door-to-door Bible salesmen).

Cinéma-vérité

Originally coined by Russian documentarist Dziga Vertov, this term came to prominence when used to describe a type of European film-making in the early 1960s (e.g. the work of Jean-Luc Godard and Jean Rouch). The term *cinéma-vérité* loosely refers to any type of film-making that uses documentary techniques, hand-held camera, a single sound microphone and interview techniques. The basic premise is that a camera and a microphone should be as near to an event as possible and the tape should be allowed to run continuously in an attempt to capture actual reality (according to Branston and Stafford the shooting ratio for *vérité* documentaries is twenty to thirty hours of film for a one hour programme). Rouch believed that by putting a camera and a microphone in front of a person and recording, the person was being given a public forum and consequently their reactions would be more sincere; it was for the film-maker to know how to take advantage of this. *Vérité* film-making can actually be traced back as far as the work of the Lumiére Brothers, whose actualities recorded the streets of Paris in a relatively unmanipulated way. Later in post-war Europe the neo-realism of film-makers such as Roberto Rossellini, Vittorio De Sica and Cesare Zavattini, inspired film-makers to use real locations and attempt a greater sense of realism. This can be seen in such American films of America as **The Naked City** (Jukes Dassin, 1948) and **On the Waterfront** (Elia Kazan, 1954), as well as in the work of British directors Lindsay Anderson, Karel Reisz and Tony Richardson.

In 1960, when the portable, sync-sound was developed, *vérité* film-making really began to take off and feature length films using these techniques began to be made, such as John Cassavetes' **Shadows** (1960) and Morris Engle's **Weddings and Babies** (1960). The approach was adopted somewhat more wholeheartedly in France where anthropologist Jean Rouch and sociologist Edgar Morin together made **Chronicle of a Summer - Une Experience de Cinéma-vérité** (1960). This extremely influential documentary, photographed by the French-Canadian Brault, featured the film-makers on screen, prompting the Parisians they were interviewing with questions. The subtitle is a homage to Vertov.

The phrase '*cinéma-vérité*' is often used interchangeably with 'direct cinema'. Both were developed during the late 1950s/early 1960s and both make use of lightweight, portable cameras and sync-sound equipment to capture events as they happen on location, without the use of a script. The film-makers sought to use the camera in such a way as to reveal a deeper level of truth about the world than what Vertov called the 'imperfect human eye'. In terms of *cinéma-vérité* Rouch believed that a film-maker

Cinéma-vérité method of filming:

• the film-maker would interview his/her subjects;

• the filming would be interrupted;

• the camera acted as the tool of the filmmaker and the filmmaking process was a means to explore their subjects' preoccupations.

ought to present an argued point of view in their work and was able to do so because the camera was far more accurate than a human eye and it also had a better memory. This led to what he called 'cinema-sincerity' in that film-makers were asking their audience to have faith in their work and the evidence being presented to them.

'[You] say to the audience, this is what I saw. I didn't fake it, this is what happened. I didn't pay anyone to fight, I didn't change anyone's behaviour. I looked at what happened with my subjective eye and this is what I believe took place.'
Jean Rouch,
Source: Kevin MacDonald and Mark Cousins, *Imagining Reality: The Faber Book of Documentary*, London: Faber, 1998, p. 265)

Few film-makers practised *cinéma-vérité* in its most pure form. However, its influence can be seen in the work of several contemporary documentarists, such as Molly Dineen and Nick Broomfield. These days '*cinéma-vérité*' is frequently used as a blanket term to describe the documentary film-making style rather than the principles of the film-makers themselves.

Molly Dineen

'It's a very intimate, personal and full-on way of working, and it can be too much for me. I've tried to make it a bit more controlled, and give it boundaries, but that doesn't work unless you start directing people, pushing them around....It's very hard living in a situation where you are absolutely aware of change and when your tendency has been to go and record it, and communicate it.'
Molly Dineen, 'Real to Reel', *The Guardian*, 17 November 2003

Already a respected film-maker for focusing on subjects or institutions living on borrowed time (e.g. London Zoo, the House of Lords) Dineen became a celebrity when her documentary on ex-Spice Girl Geri Halliwell was screened on Channel 4 at prime time (***Geri Halliwell***, 1999). In a canny piece of PR Halliwell called upon the services of Dineen when her career as a Spice Girl was coming to an end and her future as a solo singer was uncertain. The result was a candid, intimate portrait of a celebrity who was seemingly tormented by the fame she craved. The film features many telling moments (Halliwell writing to the Prince of Wales for advice but having trouble over what words to use and asking Dineen for her opinion; choosing a dog from Battersea Dogs' Home with her friend George Michael; and her 'cosmic shopping list' which she hides behind a picture in her bedroom). Dineen's filming enables the audience to gain an insight into the star that is not always flattering and at one point Halliwell argues with Dineen about who has the creative control over the film when she fears that what is being recorded will destroy her public image. (Ultimately the film proceeded on a 50:50 control basis; Halliwell had wanted 100 per cent control.)

Interestingly, Dineen's reputation as a film-maker who portrayed personalities sympathetically was a factor when the Labour Party employed her to make a short film about Tony Blair during the 1997 election campaign. The ten minute highly personalised, documentary-style election broadcast followed Blair around his home making tea, chatting to his children in the kitchen and sharing his dream as a young boy of playing for Newcastle United football team. This deliberately 'raw' presentation succeeded in the party's aim of presenting Blair as a warm human being who was a humble man of the people. Or as Peter Mandelson, the Labour Party Campaign manager, said at the time, 'This is not Blair the movie, this is Blair the man' (source: http://www.ge9/.co.uk). Labour went on to win a landslide victory at the polls.

In November 2003, Dineen won the prestigious Trustees Award (formerly the Lifetime Achievement Award) at the Grierson British Documentary Awards in recognition of her 18 years of unique, quirky film-making.

Dineen's filmography:

o ***Home From The Hill*** (BBC, 1985, 58 mins)
– a focus on Colonel Hook, a retired colonel who returns to England from Kenya. It won an RTS award, a BAFTA nomination, a BFI Grierson Award nomination and numerous other awards at documentary festivals.

o ***Operation Raleigh, The Mountain, The Village*** (BBC2, 1988, 2 x 30mins)
– an expedition to South Chile.

o ***My African Farm*** (BBC2, 1988, 40mins)
– a portrait of Sylvia Richardson and her servants on her Kenyan farm one Christmas. It won the BFI / Kodak Newcomers of the Year Award 1988 and the Prix de Bibliotheques, Lyon Biennale Europeane de Cinema 1989.

o ***Heart of the Angel*** (BBC2, 1989, 40mins)
– a look at a London underground station. It won an RTS award, was nominated for the BFI Grierson Award and was the British entry for Prix Europa.

o ***The Pick, The Shovel and The Open Road*** (C4, 1990, 60mins)
– a focus on McNicholas, an Irish roadwork company.

o ***The Ark*** (BBC, 1992, 4 x 1hr)
– London zoo in crisis across a six month period. It won a BAFTA, Special Commendation at the Prix Europa, Voice of Viewers and Listeners Best Television Programme 1993 award and the Documentaries and Features Award at the Indies 1994.

o ***In the Company of Men*** (BBC, 1995, 3 x 1hr)
– a focus on Welsh Guards serving In Northern Ireland.

o ***Tony Blair*** (1997, 10mins)
– Labour Party election broadcast.

o ***Geri*** (C4, 1999, 90mins)
– profile of ex-Spice Girl Geri Halliwell in the 3 months following her
  departure from the band.

o ***The Lord's Tale*** (C4, 2002, 75 mins)
– focus on the reform of the House of Lords.

Interestingly, in her book *New Documentary: A Critical Introduction*, Stella
Bruzzi considers the work of Dineen (alongside that of Nick Broomfield and
Jon Ronson) and defines their work as 'performative documentary' in that all
of these film-makers allow their presence to be known in front of the camera,
which ultimately (arguably) affects the outcome of the film. This presence
underlines the fact that the documentary is a different version of reality, one
which is based upon encounters between the film-maker, their subject and
the audience.

Direct cinema and *cinéma-vérité*

Similarities

Valued intimacy, immediacy and 'the real'

Rejected the glossy aesthetic of traditional cinema

Unconcerned by grainy, wobbly pictures

Any flaws (such as a momentary lapse in focus) reinforced authenticity

Differences

Different opinions on the issue of the film-makers intervention

Cinéma-vérité believed that the camera could reveal a truer representation of the world than the human eye

Cinéma-vérité used interviews to get opinions across; direct cinema eschewed interviews entirely

'The direct cinema documentarist took his camera to a situation of tension and waited hopefully for a crisis; the Rouch version of cinéma-vérité tried to precipitate one. The direct cinema artist aspired to invisibility; the Rouch cinéma-vérité artist was often an avowed participant. The direct cinema artist played the role of uninvolved bystander; the cinéma-vérité artist espoused that of provocateur ... Direct cinema found its truth in events available to the camera. Cinéma-vérité was committed to a paradox: that artificial circumstances could bring hidden truth to the surface.'
Erik Barnouw
A History of Non-Fiction Film, New York: Oxford University Press, 1993, p. 254-5

Regardless of these distinctions both *vérité* and direct cinema film-makers believe in what Rouch called the 'privileged moment'; a moment during the filming of events as they happen, when the truth about the subject is revealed. This moment tends to take place during an interview when the interviewee becomes suddenly aware, for the first time, of the truth behind the situation, often provoking great empathy from the audience. To what extent the camera manipulates this moment is a controversial issue and one which is hotly debated.

British Television Documentary

'... [there is a] spirit of inquiry at the heart of the UK's
documentary tradition.'
Steve Hewlett, ITV
From an interview:
www.bbc.co.uk/info/bbc/gov_seminar_birt.shtml

The Post-war Years

Britain, like America, turned to television as a platform for
the non-fiction film in the post-war period. Up to that
point television had been slow to adopt the genre as
most of the early television schedules comprised 'live'
programmes and documentaries took weeks, perhaps
months, of filming, followed by an equally long editing
period. By now TV was making an impact on cinema box
office and so documentaries began to be shown in the
home rather than on the big screen.

A key motivating factor for this move towards television
was to take advantage of the still prevalent Reithian
philosophy of the medium as a public service institution,
as well as providing the much-needed production
funding for the industry. An additional factor was the
introduction of the 16mm lightweight, hand-held camera
which enabled greater mobility, a more intimate
relationship between the camera and its subject and,
consequently, a greater sense of realism and immediacy.

In the 1950s one of the first key figures to be associated
with the genre was Denis Mitchell, who made several
documentaries for the BBC, including **Morning in the
Streets** (a study of the people of Salford), **Night in the
City** (a study of the desolation experienced during the
hours of darkness) and **In Prison**. The rhythms and
vocabulary of everyday speech fascinated Mitchell and he

allowed his subjects to speak for themselves. Prior to working in television he produced a series of 'sound documentaries' for BBC radio, where he recorded sounds while standing on street corners with a tape recorder. Working in television Mitchell attempted to capture a certain sense of sadness as well as passion, but in a less stylised fashion than had hitherto been experienced in the documentaries of the 1930s. Mitchell avoided the use of a script or a narrator, preferring instead to be spontaneous and hope for the best, while avoiding any deliberate subtext or message. This certainly worked during the filming of *Night in the City* when, while Mitchell was filming him on a bombsite, a man confessed to a murder he had committed.

In the early days of TV documentary budgets were small, with little or no money spent on presenters. However, by the early 1960s documentaries had become more ambitious and prestigious, with big name journalists and academics now employed to lend weight to the programmes as well as to steer the audience through the complexities of the subject matter. For example in 1969, the art historian, Kenneth Clarke, charted the history of Western civilisation in a thirteen part series called *Civilisation*. This was followed by *The Ascent of Man*, a groundbreaking Natural History series from the BBC fronted by Jacob Bronowski and commissioned by the then Head of BBC2 David Attenborough, who would go on to almost single-handedly invent the wildlife documentary sub-genre.

One problem faced by documentary film-makers when dealing with TV is that the TV networks have to adhere to their own charter (i.e. a commercial, political and moral agenda). Thus the network may reject a documentary if they perceive its content to contravene the charter in some way. A good example of this occurred in 1965 when Peter Watkins made a docudrama, *The War Game*, which showed the effects of a nuclear explosion on London. It was felt to be too politically sensitive to broadcast and was not screened until 1985, twenty years after it was made.

7 Up (Michael Apted, 1964)

Since 1964 Michael Apted has recorded the lives of a group of British people at seven-year intervals. Apted's initial intention was purely to document the schoolchildren's lives just the once, but the project grew to the extent that the series has become the most famous in television documentary history.

The first film was conceived and transmitted as a one-off programme for the **World in Action** series on ITV to look at the 'shop stewards and executives of the future', with the agenda very much about the class system. At that time the class that people were born into largely predetermined people's life chances. Apted was given the responsibility of finding twelve children whose parents would be willing for them to be the focus of a documentary. Given that he only had ten days in which to achieve this task the majority of children came from London, with one child from Liverpool, one from Yorkshire, one non-white and only four (out of the twelve) girls - hardly a balanced demographic spread! (The American and Russian versions of the documentary, which Apted produces, are much more representative of their respective populations.)

While the series has subsequently charted the lives of these children, at sevenyear intervals, through adolescence and into adulthood, it has also become a fascinating insight into the political and social history of post-war Britain, making it an important historical text. The subjects' developing views on their
lives as seen in the programmes are intercut with the current reality of their situation. We have observed the group going through the universal process of growing up, getting a job, having a family and getting old. Interestingly, as Bruce, Neil, Suzy et al. have grown older and more independent, Apted has experienced difficulty in convincing them to participate in the documentary every seven years; the documentation of their lives having become just too invasive for some of them.

Such is the viewing public's interest in this style of documentary that in April 2000 a new version of the series was launched. Adhering to the original style, **7 Up 2000** again focuses on the lives of a group of seven-year-olds but this time the director, Julian Farino, is waiting to see what the potent issue raised by the programme might be. Apted, who is a consultant on the new series, believes that class is no longer such an issue as it was when he began the series in 1964.

Apted's feature film directing credits include: ***Triple Echo*** (1973), ***Stardust*** (1975), ***The Coal Miner's Daughter*** (1980), ***Gorillas in the Mist*** (1988), Nell (1994) and ***The World is Not Enough*** (1999).
His other documentary credits include ***Bring on the Night*** (1985), ***28 Up*** (1985), ***35 Up*** (1991) and ***42 Up*** (1998).

Another factor which had (and still has) an impact on whether or not a documentary was broadcast was the ongoing ratings war fought between the TV networks. To guarantee good ratings TV has to be of interest to the highest possible audience segment which usually means that it must be entertaining or 'sexy'. By virtue of being based on fact this may be difficult for a documentary, especially when it makes demands on its audience in terms of requiring them to form opinions. While the recent spate of TV documentaries do not necessarily garner high audiences, they have moved away from the traditional 'selfimprovement' values associated with the genre to focus on topics that are entertaining and of interest to the public (e.g. neighbours who fight in ***Neighbours at War***, the clubbing scene in ***Ibiza Uncovered***, examples of bad driving in ***So You Think You Are a Good Driver?***).

British TV Documentary Today

'I don't know where documentary is going but at the moment it is fast becoming a soap opera in order to keep its place in the schedules...'
Molly Dineen,
Source: Kevin MacDonald and Mark Cousins, *Imagining Reality: The Faber Book of Documentary*, London: Faber, 1998, p. 366

Because they are dealing with the 'real', documentaries are very much part of public service broadcasting and therefore a feature of our democracy (i.e. they exercise people's freedom of speech). In England, Channel 4 was the first terrestrial TV channel to commit to feature length documentaries (the *True Stories* series which ran for ten years), despite their perceived imposition on scheduling. C4's policy for documentaries advocates the importance of the genre in giving rise to the expression by a variety of authors from a broad range of film-making backgrounds, while also acknowledging the diverse interests and backgrounds of the channel's audience.

In today's TV schedules we now accept documentaries as commonplace. Indeed they have proven to be so popular that a number of sub-genres have developed. For example **institutional documentaries** have picked up on the techniques of direct cinema, using technology to focus on institutions which affect our daily lives, offering the inquisitive audience an insight into the inner workings and characters who populate them (e.g. *Police*, based at the Thames Valley force; *Hong Kong Beat*, based in the colony's HQ; *Jimmy's*, based in St James Hospital, Leeds; *Children's Hospital*, based in London's Great Ormond Street). This popular genre is often informative or humorous and sometimes critical in the way in which these places of work are represented.

New technology has meant that anyone can make a documentary and this has led to a proliferation of **video diary** documentaries which might look amateur but succeed in combining a sense of honesty and intimacy, with very little production interference. Another descendant of the direct cinema ethos, these have proven to be an extremely popular format among the viewing public who see this extension of the genre as more truthful since the subject is filming themselves (see p.57). Other programmes which use surveillance technology as entertainment (e.g. ITV's *Police, Camera, Action*) are also extremely popular with the viewing public who seem to enjoy their voyeuristic nature. An even newer form of unmediated video production is available via the internet on websites which use webcams to record and broadcast live the daily lives of ordinary people, particularly women.

'I don't think we can, or should, think of there being different categories; I think they're all part of the body of documentary. We can't dismiss as entertainment, though they may be entertaining, programmes such as The House, Hotel, Driving School, HMS Brilliant and a dozen more, and not just the BBC. These frankly are brilliant programmes; they offer acute insights, they reflect our times, they tell us tellingly how life is lived in the United Kingdom and around the world today. And they're going to be an extraordinary text for future historians.'

Sir John Birt, ex-Director General, BBC

From an interview featured on www.bbc.co.uk/info/bbc/gov_seminar_birt.shtml

*'Low budget entertainment doesn't come any cheaper.
The police traffic videos featured in last September's
documentary* Police Stop! *proved to be the highest
rating programme of 1994.'*
(*The Observer*, 20 December 1994)

Docusoaps

Every major terrestrial channel in the UK is currently
investing money in factual TV. Long a staple of UK
television, factual programmes are now a key feature of
any prime-time schedule. One of the main reasons for
this is the massive popularity of the docusoap. British
television has become saturated with docusoaps,
following everyone from hotel owners to vets to wheel
clampers. It would seem that no job is too small, or too
boring, to become the focus of prime-time television and
the British public just can't seem to get enough of them.

Docusoaps take ordinary, common experience and look
at it through the eyes of the public. This sub-genre
adopts the documentary form and combines it with an
entertainment agenda - a technique often called
'infotainment'. However, the programmes make an
impression upon the audience by virtue of the fact that
they are employing conventions we associate with the
documentary genre and its claims and beliefs about
reality.

Programme makers have unearthed extraordinary
personalities in ordinary jobs (e.g. Jeremy Spake in ***Airport***;
Eileen in ***Hotel***; Ray Brown in ***Clampers***; Herbert in
Shampoo). These people have become household names
with agents and fans. For many, doors have been opened
and new careers in entertainment have been launched. For
example, after the success of ***Airport*** Jeremy Spake went
on to appear on ***Blankety Blank***, a special edition of
Children's Hospital, he is currently writing a book and
has plans to make a programme about his grandmother
who was an interpreter for Stalin. Similarly, Trude from
Vets in Practice has had her own show and has even
appeared on a set of Royal Mail stamps, dressed as a

fairy, and Ray from **Clampers** went on to star as an alternative Cilla Black on a gay blind date programme.

According to Brian Winston (in his essay 'The Primrose Path: Faking TV Documentary, "Docuglitz" and Docusoap', 1998) the current level of popularity for documentaries is a new phenomenon, and docusoaps have been the vehicle for this success. The mainstream documentary tradition has tended towards sober examinations of the world around us with programmes not expected (or required) to be big hits, commercially. The less-serious tone and style of docusoaps has made the documentary more popular even as their more frivolous approach has been much criticised. However, in its favour the genre does at least celebrate its characters rather than portray them as victims, and does employ humour in its delivery, while informing us about Britain and the British. It is this, plus its use of strong, interesting and illuminating characters that has helped garner popular appeal and ensure that other countries have bought the programmes (i.e. programmes such as **The Cruise**, **HMS Brilliant**, **Children's Hospital** and **Airport** have been bought in the States, Europe, Australia and Canada).

The relationship between the press and the docusoaps is an interesting one. While critics are quick to savage many of them, the same newspapers are running features elevating their stars to celebrity status. For example, the castaway Ray on **Castaway 2000** had the tabloids falling over themselves to help him get off the island and have exclusive rights to his version of life on Taransay. More seriously, critics have accused film-makers of contriving or recreating situations and events and passing them off as real and some have indeed been exposed as including faked scenes (e.g. **Driving School** for BBC1 in 1997; **Daddy's Girl** for Channel 4 in 1998).

'The docusoap format has given us more than enough opportunities for social voyeurism and sneery divisiveness, not that most of us need any excuse to play the national sport.'
Kathryn Flett,
The Observer, 16 January 2000

Conventions of docusoaps:

• they tend to be a multi-part series;

• topics tend to be banal or everyday;

• feature a number of strong, hyperbolic personalities;

• the characters stories are interwoven;

• characters 'play-up' to the camera;

• the programmes incorporate elements of melodrama and end on a cliffhanger (a convention of a soap opera);

• programmes are comparatively cheap to produce;

• programmes appear very structured;

• the shooting style appears informal (e.g. characters often make asides to the camera, over their shoulder).

Drama-documentaries

A booklet published by Granada in 1980, the 'Woodhead Doctrine', aimed to clarify what a 'drama-doc' was. Named after Leslie Woodhead, a producer of numerous dramadocs for Granada himself, the doctrine stated,

> *'The aim of a dramatised documentary is to recreate as accurately as possible history as it happened. No invented characters, no invented names, no dramatic devices owing more to the writer's (or director's) creative imagination than to the implacable record of what actually happened. For us, the dramatised documentary is an exercise in journalism, not dramatic art.'*

It was Granada that pioneered this form. While some dramatists tried to ape current affairs conventions, they borrowed from the traditions of drama. Granada produced such programmes as: ***The Man Who Couldn't Keep Quiet*** (1970) based on the story of Grigorenko, a Soviet dissident; ***Three Days in Szezecin*** (1976), a reconstruction of the Polish shipyard strike; ***Invasion*** (1980), an account of the crushing of the Prague Spring; and ***Strike*** (1981), based on the Gdansk strike of 1980 which had given rise to the establishment of the Solidarity movement in Poland.

However, this format was not without its critics. Indeed, the 1980 drama-doc ***Death of a Princess***, made for ITV by Anton Thomas, courted widespread controversy. The programme was a dramatised version of the execution of a princess in Saudi Arabia, found guilty of adultery, a 'crime' punishable by death. The programme also featured a character who represented Thomas himself, analysing the rumours surrounding the story. The criticism aimed at the programme was largely due to what some saw as Thomas's negative representation of the Saudi government and culture. Reports published at the time claimed that Britain lost £200 million of business with Saudi Arabia as a consequence of the film and the then Foreign Secretary, Lord Carrington had to personally apologise to the Saudi leaders.

BBC Video Diaries

'We are a species in love with its own moving image.'
Paul Barker,
Source: Kevin MacDonald and Mark Cousins, *Imagining Reality: The Faber Book of Documentary*, London: Faber, 1998, p. 357

Screened on BBC2, this series consists of short, intensely personal essays, in which non-film-makers (actual members of the public) who have a story to tell are given a camcorder to record it. This is then edited to create an often intriguing fly-on-the-wall documentary. What is interesting is that a non-professional with little-to-no expertise can capture a significant moment in his/her life and create meaning for an audience. Thus the average person on the street can be the creator as well as the subject and the audience, giving a voice to members of the public that have hitherto been ignored.

The series is produced by the BBC's Community Programmes Unit, the concept for it originating as a direct result of the increasing success (in terms of the quality of the picture and the decrease in price) of the newly developed camcorder, in particular the high-quality format (i.e. Hi-8 camera) in the early 90s. This piece of equipment enables longer takes and an uninterrupted shoot. In addition, you do not have to be an expert to use one and they create a great sense of intimacy.

The key motivating factors behind the commissioning of the *Video Diaries* programmes are that they are cheap to make and are ideally suited as 'fillers' between programmes. Once a Video Diary idea is decided upon the diarist receives basic training in 'the grammar of television' and the editor helps the person to focus their ideas. However the diarist does have the right to veto any decision. According to the programme's editor, Jeremy Gibson,

'this little camera ... shows up the unfortunate methods of most fly-on-the-wall TV: the kerfuffle, the time, the crew. You can use this without threatening other people.'
Source: ibid., p. 355

Recent audience figures showed that audiences for *Video Diaries* have reached around one million viewers. Such was the success of the programme that the BBC commissioned a variant of the format, *Teenage Diaries*, some of which have been seen by one and a half million viewers.

Traditionally, documentaries were produced for the big screen and made for a cinema audience. Television has made an enormous contribution to the development of the genre but has diminished it too, since very few actually get a theatrical release these days. However, with the increase in cable TV, the video market and the Internet, changes in TV programming and consumption are inevitable. Today there is much more choice available to the consumer (some might say too much choice) and some channels are totally dedicated to the documentary genre (e.g. The Discovery Channel screens documentaries worldwide). With the digital explosion and the introduction of interactive TV, programmers can afford to be more progressive and ambitious in their decisions. There now appears to be virtually no subject that hasn't been touched by documentaries. It appears there will always be an audience who want to see how the world works without leaving the comfort of their own surroundings.

Reality TV

'...television can act as fairy godmother... it can change not only their rooms, but their jobs, skin colour (temporarily) and sex (superficially). It can swap wives, transport families to new lives in Brisbane or Brighton, and put couples on a character-testing trek through the Namibian desert. It can take them back to live in 1900 or 1940, or below stairs in an Edwardian country house. And above all it can make them very famous.*

David Liddiment,

'Reality TV's Ultimate Trick', The Guardian, 28 April 2003

Discussion point:

Is reality TV about control, power and interaction?

Is it a scientific experiment?

Is it a good excuse for 'a nose'?

Some contemporary textual examples of reality television:

Popstars, Jailbreak, The 1940s House, Surviving the Iron Age, Shipwrecked, Temptation Island, Wife Swap, Boss Swap, Celebrity Big Brother, Boot Camp, Bar Wars, The Salon *and* Shattered *to name but a few.*

In a recent interview in the *Radio Times*, veteran broadcaster Barry Norman, criticised the BBC for lowering its standards and submitting to the 'lurid appeal' of the populist genre of reality TV. Norman argued that such programmes were easy scheduling and claimed that the BBC were cashing in on the genre's appeal, motivated by the ratings war instead of on delivering programmes of quality (as required under the strictures of Public Service Broadcasting).

Nevertheless, it is the fact that reality TV shows are a highly successful format in the world of television is not to be ignored. The shows are part of our common parlance – everyone talks about them. This is borne out by the fact that, like them or loath them, there are very few people in our society who don't know who Jade Goody or 'Nasty' Nick Bateman are. For the likes of Jade and Nick, reality TV shows are springboards into the world of fame (albeit a temporary C-list type of fame). It is for this very reason that showbiz has-beens are beating a path to appear on reality TV programmes such as ITV's *I'm A Celebrity Get Me Out of Here* or Channel 4's *Celebrity Big Brother*, the shows are so popular that they are an excellent quick-fix way of rejuvenating your career. Who would have thought that Peter Andre would grace our pop charts ever again after his original success in the 90s? After his music career dwindled to nil he went to work in his brother's gym before appearing on *I'm A Celebrity Get Me Out of Here* in early 2004, during which his antics with glamour model and all-round party girl Jordan, ensured him a lot of tabloid column inches and a re-entry into the pop charts with *Insania*.

Most terrestrial television channels now have several reality TV shows as a regular feature in their schedules essentially because (a) they are comparatively cheap to produce and (b) they are such a draw with audiences and ratings are the key to success for all production companies; they are a commercial imperative. Indeed, a recent Ofcom survey showed that the total volume of viewing of factual entertainment (i.e. reality TV shows) had grown by as much as 20 per cent between 1998 and 2002, with the largest increase on Channel 4. This is most marked when one considers that during the same period, the volume of viewing of serious factual programming fell dramatically by almost 10 hours per head, a decrease of 36 per cent; the majority of this decline was felt by BBC1, who had significantly reduced its peak-hour scheduling of popular serious factual programming. The Ofcom report suggests that audiences today are not what they used to be in terms of size and we need to consider two very important points:

1) TV is a much more competitive market than it used to be say ten years ago and;
2) audiences today are increasingly 'cash rich and time poor', they demand instant fixes from the television viewing in today's ever-pressurised world.

Audiences preoccupation with the 'cult of celebrity' means that reality TV shows are an ideal solution to this last point; they provide immediate gossip and voyeuristic value.

A hybrid form of television documentary, reality TV shows bring together a group of nobodies, people who are carefully chosen to represent 'ordinary people' but who the producers believe will make highly watchable television; there is something about these people's personality or look, that will encourage viewers to want to watch them. For a pre-determined period of time these people enter our lives at a certain time on a particular channel. They are often pigeonholed into certain character roles, be it bully, loser or femme fatale; each programme carefully constructed to position an audience to make judgements on these people who they don't know. The programme's narrative will be edited to provoke a particular response and great use is made of narrative tension to encourage audiences to stay tuned. Soon we find ourselves, sometimes against our better judgement, intrigued by them...we feel over a period of time that we have grown to know them and, inexplicably, we start to debate their actions and merits with our friends (and sometimes total strangers).

What then can we say are the ingredients or 'generic conventions' of this highly successful, marketable product?

Points to consider:
• ironically reality TV is not very 'real';
• the situations are highly contrived;
• the protagonists are handpicked to fulfil a particular function;
• what we see is extremely manipulated, an endless parade of highly selected images. No-one (whether they are viewing online or on TV) sees *everything* that is seen by the cameras - what is streamed is already edited (mediated).

So, reality TV programmes can therefore be argued to generate their own 'mini-reality', with their own highly artificial rules and values.

Contestants are there because they have volunteered but there are people / programme producers (who are careful to remain anonymous) who are pulling the contestants' strings. The contestants may say what they please but someone else will decide what we, the

Discuss the above comment made by a journalist in relation to I'm A Celebrity Get Me Out of Here. To what extent do agree with his opinion?

viewer, actually see and hear. For this reason, reality TV isn't really a form of voyeurism – as our victim's are fully aware they are being watched – they gave their consent when they entered the programme and signed their contract with the production company.

Many reality TV programmes ensure their presence is known by seeking a significant amount of attention from other mediums. Gaining a high profile with their target audience via other media texts that share that audience is essential to gain the all-important television ratings and advertising revenue.

Let's consider then the cross-media fertilization that surrounded Channel 4's series ***Big Brother 2*** (2001):

The Internet
Many websites – both official and unofficial – arose around the time of the series being aired. Below are just some of them.

www.bigbrother.terra.com - official site
www.bigbrotherworld.com - how the programme transpires globally
www.channel4.co.uk/bigbrother – official channel site dedicated to the programme
www.bigbrotheronline.co.uk - voting, chat, games, trivia
www.unofficialbigbrother.co.uk - an alternative voice
www.orwellproject.com – reality TV dedicated site with casting calls, fan pages, hotlinks to programmes
www.bigbrother.fanspace.com – fans website
www.bigbrotherlover.com– fans website
www.bigsister.fsnet.co.uk – spin-off
www.sirlinksalot.net/ukbigbrother.html – fast links to various BB links
http://bigbrother.thelukester.com –unofficial site
www.bigbrotherboyz.com - for fans of the male contestants
www.briandowling.net – for fans
www.bigmummafreak.com – alternative voice

www.envy.nu/narinder – her official appreciation site
www.bigbrotherpaul.tripod.com – the Paul-must-win site!
www.somersetorganics.co.uk - on-line voting for your least favourite pig to raise money for foot & mouth disease victims

Sponsorship and Product Placement

- BT Cellnet – the official **Big Brother** sponsor who banked on viewers using the premium rate services available. And in an experiment in mass market entertainment messaging, die-hard **BB** fans could buy pre-pay Cellnet vouchers to receive a range of messages and services for **Big Brother** (the original **Big Brother** series was sponsored by Southern Comfort).
- *Heat* magazine – party ticket offer for the last night; saturation coverage.
- Ryan Air – Good luck message for Brian emblazoned on the side of one of their fleet's Boeing 737 aircraft. Ryan Air also pledged to donate £1000 to the NSPCC for every week that Brian spent in the house.
- IKEA – provided furniture in the house.

Newspaper and magazine coverage (good example of intertextuality – i.e. references to other media texts)

There was severe competition as any coverage was a guaranteed sales coup and there was some interesting (and at times tenuous) coverage. It is important to remember that the summer is conventionally a slow news period.

- *The Sun* / *News of the World* / Dominic Mohan provided saturation front page splash approach. In a deal said to be worth £40,000 the paper backed Bubble, who went on to be the fourth evictee:

'*The Sun Backs Bubble*…this is a momentous announcement – the biggest since we backed Tony Blair in the 1997 General Election – and we have not taken it

Such was the success of RDF Media's Wife Swap, that Channel 4 screened an alternative Queen's speech on Christmas Day 2003, featuring two of the more 'interesting' characters from the series – Michelle and Barry Seaborn from Southport.

lightly…Together we can blow him to victory.'

Later, *The Sun* supported Helen Adams who they depicted as a working-class hero.

When the *News of the World* ran a world exclusive on Helen the bottom of the article was stamped in bold with the words 'Copyright News of the World 2001. Our lawyers are watching'.

- *The Mirror* ('*The Official* Big Brother *paper*') / *Sunday Mirror* / *Daily Express* / *Daily Star* all ran 'exclusive' stories on Helen and Paul's romance. Interestingly, *The Mirror* in 1999 ran several outraged articles about the popular Channel 4 gay-themed drama **Queer as Folk**, and yet such was the draw of **BB** (in terms of people buying papers for snippets of news on the prog and its contestants) that the self-same paper ran the headline '*We're Coming Out for Brian*' urging its readers to vote for him to win. *OK!* magazine (which is owned by the same people as the *Express*) also ran stories on Josh and Paul.

- In a similar about-face, *The Daily Mail* initially disliked **Big Brother** and Brian Dowling as a person. Nevertheless, such was the draw of the programme that it was cowed into publishing a photo of Brian as he left the house the overall winner, the paper feared alienating readers if it did not report the moment.

Merchandise
Products affiliated with the show, which could be ordered via a 24 hrs hotline and web site – www.buybigbrother.com – included a DVD, CD soundtrack, mugs, shot glasses, 'Uncut' video, board game, T-shirts galore, hats, bags, accessories, disposable cameras, Nokia mobile phone cover and mouse mat.

C4 Television

- **Little Brother** – bringing people up to date with happenings in the house via a team with no previous experience and a budget of £25 per day.
- E4 live stream – prior to **BB2** E4 hadn't officially registered an audience as there needs a minimum of 50,000 viewers for a programme for it to be recorded. But the live stream was a massive success – at its peak E4 was registering 1 million viewers, especially around 11–11.30pm.

Other TV show appearances:

Contestants began being marketed as a media commodity in and of themselves. For example, Helen was marketed as a 'ditzy blonde' who loved glitter and was seen on numerous terrestrial television shows, including **SM: TV** (ITV1), **Celebrity Ready Steady Cook** (BBC2), **Lorraine Kelly** (ITV1), **So Graham Norton** (C4). The promise of audience figures had rival channels paying for the ex-contestants to make a guest appearance on their shows.

The contestants became (albeit temporarily) a part of popular culture and their language and expressions become part of our mode of expression – e.g. '*I love glitter, I do*' (Helen); '*Evil!*' (Brian); '*I live the life of an international pop star*' (Paul – something I'm sure he regrets saying now).

Big Brother 2 vs. Survivor: a tale of two reality TV series

Summer 2001 was the 'summer of reality television' where TV bosses were fighting hard to woo viewers to stay in and watch their programme. **Big Brother 2** and **Survivor** were the heavyweight contenders. Both shows concerned very modern dilemmas; thrown together by circumstances, the contestants were mutually dependent on one another, but in order to survive they had to stab one another in the back by making nominations for eviction.

Series 7: The Contenders (2001) (cert 18) (87mins)
Dir. Daniel Minahan

Interestingly, this action film was marketed in the UK using the tagline 'Big Brother With Bullets'. The storyline took the notion behind reality TV one step further. The film depicts a reality TV show, set in America, where the contestants are engaged in a city-wide game of cat-and-mouse in which the objective is to kill one another at any cost to win the show's prize.

Survivor was a new programme which had been a roaring success in the USA with contestants abandoning all morals and forming sneaky alliances. It had high production values, was set on an exotic island with blue seas and sunlit skies, had scantily clad contestants who had to think tactically and battle with their consciences for a whopping £1 million prize money. The programme offered filmed images, emotional suffering and tribal councils.

Big Brother 2 on the other hand wasn't new. The original series had been a huge success for Channel 4 in 2000, hence the decision to repeat the programme with a few changes to the original format. The *Big Brother 2* house was set in a desolate part of London and the show essentially depicted a group of show-offs locked in a bungalow watched by multiple video cameras, living in an artificial world, doing very little all day apart from the occasional trivial challenge. Where was the fun in that?

But, despite early proclamations to the contrary, at the end of the day *Big Brother 2* won the battle, and it won by a mile. Why didn't *Survivor* translate across the Atlantic? That the live nature of Big Brother won-out confirms that broadcast television's fundamental strength lies in its intimate connection with the lives of its viewers.

So let's compare the formats:

Big Brother 2 vs. Survivor

	Big Brother 2	Survivor
Concept	11 contestants live in a prefabricated house with 33 secret cameras (some capable of 390 degree angles) filming their every move through two-way mirrors for 9 weeks. Each week the contestants secretly nominate 2 'housemates' for eviction. The nation decides by telephone voting. In addition the show is screened 24 hrs a day on the website and 21 hrs a day on E4.	16 contestants are divided into two tribes – the Ular and the Helang. They gradually vote each other off the tropical island each night. They are underfed and compete for food, drink & shelter as well as having to complete a number of tough physical challenges. The contestants vote to remove one of their numbers from the contest. Slogan – *Don't trust anyone.*
Origins of the concept	Based on the Dutch version- originally glossed as a social / anthropological experiment – what would contestants do if left to their own devices?	Based on the US version.
When scheduled	Commencing Bank Holiday Monday 28 May 'til the grand finale on Friday 3 August 2001 – a total of 65 programmes.	The show was pre-recorded in Borneo for ten weeks, with audiences viewing the show three weeks after their return. A special preview show to introduce the concept was aired 20 May. The final 2 contestants did a 'head-to- head' show at the end of the series with the winner, Charlotte Hobrough winning the vote 7-0.
Duration	10 weeks.	6 weeks (although the action took place across 10 weeks).
Where scheduled	E4 continuously 'live'; Channel 4 daily at 6.30pm and twice nightly on Fridays at 8pm and 10.30pm.	ITV in a primetime every Monday, Tuesday Thursday and Friday for three weeks. This was later cutback to once a week.
Location	A 'top security' house in Bromley-by-Bow, London.	Pulau Tiga, an island off the coast of Borneo in the South China Sea.
Prize	£70,000.	£1million.
Reason to watch	The house contains an interesting social mix of people and there is always the promise of the 'crying and shagging factor'.	The idea that contestants will choose money over friendship. The group was not such a varied social mix with most hailing from middle-class professions.
Target audience	'the under 30s'.	16 – 34 year old demographic.

Interestingly, Channel 4 did screen a couple (Jade Dyer and Tommy Wright, both 18 years old at the time) having sex in an offshoot of the main series, Teen Big Brother *(which aired in October 2003). The programme differed from the main series in that it was marketed as an educational experiment and was scheduled to air in the mid-morning '4 Learning' school slot; the educational angle came from the fact that the group of teenagers would be challenged, whilst co-habiting for 10 days, by a range of issues including citizenship, leadership, status, living and learning together. However, when the programme got underway hormones got in the way and the footage was so entertaining that the Channel 4 bosses decided to air the programme in the 10pm weekday slot, every night, to maximise audience potential.*

Critical success factors of *Big Brother 2*

- There is no doubt that **Big Brother** was (and continues to be) a roaring success for Channel 4 / E4. **BB2** raked in millions of pounds in telephone voting lines, scored valuable ratings to guarantee strong advertising revenue and achieved the Holy Grail of 'talked about television'.
- The programme originated in Holland: 100 days spent in a specially contrived house, with a contestant evicted every 2 weeks and no attempt at a storyline. It was a tried and tested formula.
- Channel 4 (under Chief Executive Ruth Wrigley) wanted to make it more accessible and interesting to their audience, than had happened in the original series. The changes made included: an eviction every week; a shorter/sharper format, a more stylish house; and a 'storyline' created by editing 24 hours surveillance to 24 minutes each night – it was a whole new way of doing television with a strong format.
- **Big Brother** is a 'live' television series with a good blend of character types and low production values.
- Activity within the confines of the set is minimal, with housemates set a weekly task for which they gambled their weekly food allowance.
- Contestants had the opportunity to 'offload' in the diary room (drunk or sober); these confessionals proved to be a definite selling point.
- The fact that the nation was able to vote to evict the housemates meant that viewers had a pro-active role, which left them feeling as if their actions made a difference.
- The weekly evictions became the source of national speculation and gossip on television, in the newspapers and gossip magazines.
- National newspapers (tabloids and broadsheets) covered the housemates constantly. The 'redtops' were at saturation point, with stories about the programme and the housemates private lives frequently dominating the front pages of the papers. Journalists

would also attempt to influence the audiences voting by sharing with their readers who their favourite contestants were.

- Live coverage via E4 and the web intensified the audiences experience – viewers revelled in the tedium of watching the housemates sleep, sunbathe and eat…just in case something happened.

- The show offered *thrill television* where no-one knew what would happen next and the audience felt that they could affect the outcome. Bear in mind that Britain remains the only country to have embraced a version of **Big Brother** that has never featured any explicit sexual activity (at the time of writing).

- Interestingly, **Big Brother** flopped in the US due to bad 'miscasting' and having the evictions fortnightly rather than weekly.

- It is a sign of the times that over 56,000 people applied to be on the show and that more people voted to eliminate contestants from **Big Brother 2** than voted for the present government. People are happier to observe, judge and condemn their fellow human being on capricious, partial evidence.

So what conclusions can be drawn from our comparison of **Big Brother 2** and **Survivor**?

Both shows contain a very modern dilemma. Thrown together by circumstances, the contestants are mutually dependent but in order to survive they have to stab each other in the back by making nominations for eviction. And we, the audience, are complicit in this, we watch with vicarious pleasure.

But does this make us voyeurs? Not in the literal sense as the contestants are aware that we are watching. But, according to John Ellis, it can be argued that we are positioned as *narrative voyeurs*, in that we know more than the characters do. Editing manipulates the viewers to see things from a certain angle, in a particular room, with particular characters and we see what they don't necessarily have access to (e.g. who is saying what about whom). The male voice-over constructs our response too

Discussion questions

To what extent do you agree with Channel 4's decision to air this footage in Teen Big Brother? Do you feel that the teenagers were exploited in anyway? Do you believe that the Channel was truly motivated by an educational agenda in this off shoot of the main series?

by asking questions or pointing things out to us to draw out attention to something or somebody.

The audience are fuelled by their knowledge of the minutiae of the characters' everyday interactions as well as their private feelings or even their more unappealing habits. Both shows became what Americans call '*a water cooler event*'. In other words they are a topic of conversation that naturally comes up wherever people gather.

In **Big Brother 2**, this was taken one stage further by using the web, unedited footage could be accessed via the website or watched for 18 hours a day on Channel 4's cable / satellite channel E4. This brought a whole new dimension to the reality TV genre as it means that we now have the ability to not only watch the contestants themselves, but we can also see how the programme-makers *narrativise* the programme.

At the core of **Big Brother 2** there is a unique tension – a triangle of control.

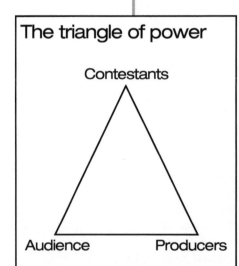

The triangle of power

Contestants

Audience   Producers

Normally in a television programme either **the contestants** control it because they are completely in charge of their destiny;

Or, **the producers** control the show via the strict rules that the contestants have to adhere to;

Or **the audience** controls it via a voting mechanism such as a phone-in.

In **Big Brother 2** there is a formatted balance of power at the heart of it. The producer can only intervene to a certain extent; the contestants can only determine their fate to a certain extent; and the audience have an element of control via their voting, but not overall. A consequence of the triangle is that each element of the triangle feels that they genuinely participate on the process.

Some important questions we need to ask ourselves are:

To what extent does **Big Brother** – or rather the contestants depicted on it - reflect our society?

Can these programmes be argued to represent a barometer of the national mood?

Can the house be said to reflect a melting pot for a broader, more understanding and inclusive society?

White, black, Asian, gay and heterosexual contestants are selected to enter the house. We watch them and get to know them; we are manipulated by the programme makers to form opinions about people that we are seduced into thinking we have come to know in some way – we judge them according to how they are represented (i.e. 're-presented' / presented again to us), by the extracts of conversation we are privy to, the moments we are witness to.

Tony Blair talks about creating a 'classless society'; John Major talked about 'creating a nation at ease with itself'. One thing which can be said about **Big Brother** is that it represents this diverse group of people optimistically – it makes the contestants almost seem at ease with their differing ethnicity, sexuality, class, religion and education.

No-one could have predicted the success of the reality TV phenomenon but now that its happened, critics and commentators tend to see it as living proof of a culture that has dumbed- down for a less literate generation with a shorter attention span. And even the television companies themselves argue that reality TV is television in its purest form – they boast that great television is all about *the trivia of the everyday*...

'Almost overnight reality TV has become the mainstay of popular culture...it is soap opera come to life.' Germaine Greer

'[Reality TV is] ...incompatible with human dignity.' Pope John Paul II

'I can't help but worry that people who take part in reality TV might be damaged in the long term.' Oliver James, psychologist

'There's no such thing as reality TV...it's rather lazily applied to tons of different formats that actually existed a long time ago...' Conrad Green, Head of Factual Entertainment, BBC / former producer on Big Brother

'The success of Big Brother confirms that broadcast television's fundamental strength lies in its intimate connection with the everyday lives of its viewers.' John Ellis, Sight and Sound

Casestudy on RDF Media

RDF Media are an interesting media institution to consider. Winner of many awards internationally, they are one of Britain's biggest independent television companies; they work in a range of television formats but are arguably most successful at producing and distributing the majority of popular reality television formats in recent television history in the UK and USA.

In business terms RDF bare one of the fastest growing media companies with an average annual growth in excess of 70 per cent over the last five years. They are also the only television company to feature in the *Sunday Times* Virgin Atlantic Fast Track 100 Companies list for the last 3 years. In 2003-04 the company's turnover was estimated at £43million.

Awards garnered by RDF Media to date include:

Montreux Rose D'Or Television Festival
Golden Rose, 2003 - *Faking It*
Press Prize, 2003 - *Faking It*
Silver Rose for Best Variety Programme, 2002 - *Perfect Match*

International Emmy Awards
Best Popular Arts Program, 2002 - *Faking It*

BAFTA - British Academy of Film & Television Arts
Best Features Programme, 2003 - *Faking It*
Best Features Programme, 2002 - *Faking It*
Best Visual Effects & Graphic Design, 2002 - *Banzai*

RTS - Royal Television Society
Best Prime Time Features Programme, 2002 - *Faking It*
Best Entertainment Programme, 2002 - *Banzai*
Best Programme By A North-West Indie, 2001 - *Drugs: The Phoney War*

Broadcast Awards
Best Independent Production Company, 2004
Best Popular Factual Programme, 2004 - *Wife Swap*
Best New Programme, 2004 - *Wife Swap*
International Programme Sales Award, 2004 - *Wife Swap*
Best Documentary Series, 2003 - *The Century Of The Self*
Best Independent Production Company, 2002

Best Popular Factual Entertainment Programme, 2002 - *Faking It*
Best New Programme, 2002 - *Banzai*
Best Multi-Channel Programme, 2002 - *Banzai*
Best Documentary, 1998 - *Tottenham Ayatollah*

Highly Commended
Best Popular Factual Programme, 2003 - *Faking It*

Indie Awards
Most Outstanding Independent Production Company (Hatrick Pioneer Award), 2003
Best Factual Programme, 2003 - *Faking It*
Best Multi-Channel Programme, 2003 - *Banzai*
Most Outstanding Independent Production Company (Hatrick Pioneer Award), 2002
Best Factual Programme, 2002 - *Faking It*
Best Light Entertainment Programme, 2002 - *Banzai*

Grierson Documentary Awards
Most Entertaining Documentary, 2002 - *Faking It* (Burger Man to Chef)

TV Quick Awards
Best Factual Programme, 2003 - *Wife Swap*

Broadcasting Press Guild
Best Single Documentary, 2003 - *Faking It* (Naval Officer to Drag Queen)

BBC One TV Moments Awards
Best Factual Moment, 2001 - *Faking It* (Burger Man to Chef)

Mental Health Media Awards
Best TV Documentary, 2000 - *Three Thin Ladies*

Howard League For Penal Reform
Media Award, 2001 - *Doing Time*

Longman-History Today Awards
Historical Film Of The Year, 2003 - *The Century Of The Self* (Programme 1)

Beijing International Scientific Film Festival
Bronze Dragon for Science Popularisation, 2000 - *Six Experiments That Changed The World*

(Source: www.rdfmedia.com)

Production history of RDF Media to date

Year	Programme title	Channel
1999	*Wheeler Dealers*	BBC2
2000	*Alt TV: Being Caprice*	Channel 4
2000	*Faking It*	Channel4
2000	*Shipwrecked*	Channel 4
2001	*Faking It – series 2 & 3*	Channel 4
2001	*Going Native*	Channel 4
2001	*Living By The Book*	Channel 4
2001	*Perfect Match*	Channel 4
2001	*Shipwrecked – series 2 & 3*	Channel 4
2001	*Shipwrecked Extra*	E4
2001	*Together Again*	Channel 4
2002	*Eden*	Channel 4
2002	*Faking It – series 4*	Channel 4
2002	*Faking It Changed My Life*	Channel 4
2002	*Perfect Match – series 2*	Channel 4
2002	*Walking With Dinosaurs*	Channel 4
2003	*Celebrity Wife Swap*	Channel 4
2003	*Fake out*	Court TV, USA
2003	*Faking It USA*	TLC & Channel 4
2003	*Holiday showdown*	ITV1
2003	*The I Do Diaries: My Best Friend's wedding*	Lifetime, USA
2003	*Masters and Servants*	Channel 4
2003	*Perfect Match, New York*	ABC Family
2003	*Trust Me, I'm A Teenager*	Channel 4
2003	*Wife Swap – series 1 & 2*	Channel 4
2003	*Wife Swap, USA (pilot)*	ABC
2003	*Wife Swap Changed Our Marriage*	Channel 4
2004	*The Block*	ITV1
2004	*Boss Swap*	Channel 4
2004	*Faking It – series 5*	Channel 4
2004	*Faking It USA – series 2*	TLC, USA
2004	*The I Do Diaries: My Best Friend's Wedding*	Lifetime, USA
2004	*Ladette to Lady*	ITV1
2004	*The Penthouse*	Sky1
2004	*Wife Swap – series 3 & 4*	Channel 4

Blurb	Duration
Entrepreneurial challenge with two teams competing to make money	4 x 30'
Just what is it like being famous? Caprice's life through a pin-hole camera	1 x 30'
Individuals are given a month to master a completely different skill and pass themselves off in front of a panel of judges	2 x 60'
A group of young people fend for themselves on a South Sea island	2 x 60' / 8 x 30'
As before	7 x 60'
A British family try to live in the African bush for 10 weeks	3 x 60'
Focus on people who agree to live by the rules / advice of self-help books	4 x 60'
Dating show where a person's mother, best friend and ex-lover choose their partner	4 x 60'
As before	24 x 30' & 1 x 60'
Behind the scenes magazine programme of the hit Channel 4 show	13 x 30'
Divorced couples agree to live together again	6 x 30'
Interactive reality show set in the Australian forest, where the lives of the cast are controlled by the viewers	39 x 30'
As before	3 x 90' & 7 x 60'
Catch-up with stars of the first three series'	1 x 60'
As before	6 x 60'
79 year old Dorothy tries to train as an air hostess	1 x 60'
Previous reality TV star Jade Goody and *Who Wants to be a Millionaire?* quiz cheat Charles Ingram, swap partners	1 x 60'
Game show about lying	6 x 30'
American version of show	5 x 60'
Two families go on holidays together for two weeks	8 x 60'
Two best friends plan each other's wedding	1 x 60'
Two families take it in turns to adopt the different roles for one another	4 x 60'
American version of the show	13 x 60'
A panel of teenage mentors try to improve peoples' lives	3 x 60'
Two very different families swap mother & wife for two weeks	4 x 60; & 6 x 60'
American version of show	1 x 60'
Catching up with previous swappers	1 x 60'
Couples compete to makeover identical properties	8 x 60'
Bosses from two separate companies swap places	4 x 60'
As before	5 x 60'
As before	13 x 60'
As before	2 x 60'
Loud-mouthed ladettes get transformed into ladies at an etiquette bootcamp	5 x 60'
Two celebrities are locked up for 24 hours in a penthouse	7 x 60'
As before	6 x 60' & 6 x 60'

For more information look at www.rdfmedia.com - RDF Media's company website

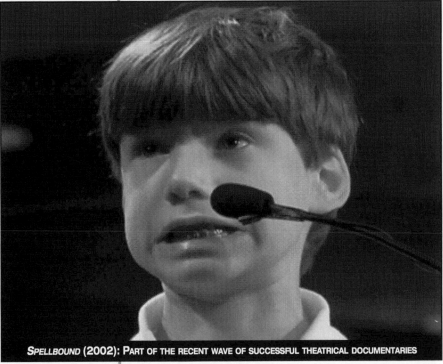

SPELLBOUND (2002): PART OF THE RECENT WAVE OF SUCCESSFUL THEATRICAL DOCUMENTARIES

Theatrical Documentaries: a renaissance story

In 2003, UK Film Council statistics revealed that cinema admissions in the UK were the second highest for 30 years*. In the fiercely competitive world of leisure, cinema is winning with audiences choosing to visit cinemas on a much more frequent basis. Interestingly, audiences' choices are widening too. In the not-too-distant past feature-length documentaries that gained a theatrical release would do so because they focused on a popular subjects such as sport – **When We Were Kings** (1996); **Hoop Dreams** (1994) – or music – **In Bed With Madonna** (1991). More recently, theatrical documentaries are beginning to gain critical acclaim and box office success, appealing to people on a much wider level. Indeed, in a review of **Capturing the Friedmans** (2003) film critic Adam Smith heralded the film as,

> 'evidence that the documentary – for so long a poor relation of the movie world – is indeed back with a vengeance.'
> **Empire, May 2004**

In recent cinema history documentaries would only have been seen in cinemas as part of special events, for a particular niche audience (e.g. archive screenings or as part of a festival, or special package of films) and most certainly not have been screened at mainstream cinemas. Nowadays, it is not unknown for theatrical documentaries to be 'must-see' movies (a phrase largely reserved for high concept / FX-ridden Hollywood studio feature fodder), with audiences able to see documentary titles at their local multiplex. Recent examples of this are **Bowling for Columbine** and the BAFTA award-winning **Touching the Void** (2003), which is currently the UK's highest grossing documentary of all time; after just 11

*London, the Midlands and Lancashire accounted for half of all UK admissions in 2003. Scotland saw 10% of all UK admissions, compared with 6.4% in Wales and West. (Source: Research and Statistics bulletin, February 2004 - www.ukfilmcouncil.org.uk)

weeks it had grossed £1,681,619. Both films achieved cross-over status, screened at both multiplexes and art house cinemas

So what is it that has heralded this shift in audiences' appreciation of theatrical documentaries? Is the fact that 'the truth is out there', seemingly literally in a factually based genre such as documentary, increasingly appealing to today's audiences? Or is it that the rise in popularity of theatrical documentary, which purports to convey reality, can be said to mirror the increase in popularity of Reality TV? Consider the comment made by film critic Adam Smith,

> *'...cinemas, the places where previous generations hunkered down, suspended their disbelief and engaged in a communal dream, are to some extent becoming refuges from the relentless artifice, places where we can go to wake up; to find out what's really going on. Or at least to engage with stories and experiences in which we believe.'*
> **Empire, May 2004**

To consider the importance of theatrical documentaries I am going to focus on two documentaries that gained a theatrical release in the UK and fared well at the box office. Quite unintentionally, but coincidentally, both films have attracted media interest and controversy for very different reasons, and they make for very interesting case studies.

The End of Innocence
Case study on *Être et avoir (To Be and To Have)*
(Cert U) (104mins)

Awards record
Prix Luois Delluc – won, 2002
Best Documentary, Valladolid International Film Festival 2002
Best Documentary, European Film Awards 2002;
Cesars 2003 – winner Best Editing;
Cesars 2003 – nominated Best Film and Best Director;

THE ENCHANTING JOJO IN ÊTRE ET AVOIR

Critics Award, French Syndicate of Cinema Critics 2003 – winner;
National Society of Film Critics, USA 2004 – winner Best Documentary;

> '*I feel badly for Nicholas Philibert...When you make a film like this, it's based on a relationship of trust between human beings – not one based on money.*'
> Director, **Christopher de Ponfilly,**
> *Screen International,* **21 November 2003**

Être et avoir is an enchanting feature-length documentary made in 2002 by renowned French director, Nicholas Philibert, using an advance on receipts subsidy from the CNC and additional financial backing from ARTE and StudioCanal. Made for $1.2 million the film went on to gross $15 million at the global box office, making it an enormous theatrical success. Not bad, one might think, for a seemingly low-key documentary which focuses on

'*My feeling is that it is not just a fashion or a trend, but that people are interested in theatrical documentaries. And that is partly because TV is so bad...you need a really bold distributor. You cannot sell a theatrical documentary in the same way as a fictional feature, with stars and so on, it takes real imagination.*'
Director, Kevin Macdonald in *Screen International,* 21 March 2003

a year in the life of a primary class in a one-room schoolhouse in Saint-Etienne Sur Usson, rural France, where a single teacher teacher, Georges Lopez, teaches all of the young children, aged 3–10. Over 1.8 million people enjoyed the film in France alone, and the firm but loving teacher, Lopez, became a national hero. His teaching style stood out as charming and old-fashioned in an age where education is increasingly pressurised the world over.

Nevertheless, in October 2003 it came to light that Lopez, rather than enjoying the film's success had filed a lawsuit against Philibert; Maia, Les Films d'Ici and Arte France Cinema (the film's producers); Les Films du Losange (the distributors); Mercure Distribution (the sales outfit) and Phillipe Hersant (the composer). The suit initially demanded £300,000 for the illegal use of his image and for counterfeiting his classes. He later extended his suit to include CanalPlus and France Television (broadcasters) and a magazine involved in promoting the film. Not satisfied with that, Lopez also bought a second case before a labour tribunal demanding pay and benefits for the time he spent travelling whilst promoting the film. Both cases are currently being tried at a Paris court and the decision is expected in 2004.

Lopez's decision certainly sent shock-waves through the documentary film-making community and clearly not only gives rise to consider the fundamental principles of documentary film-making, but also lays bare the whole concept of authorship. Regardless of the case's outcome questions are already being raised about the impact this will have on documentary film-makers' ability to raise financial backing now that there is a perceived additional risk.

Lopez claims that his actions are as a result of what he felt to be a lack of recognition. However, if one scrutinises the case in more detail one will see that the reality is somewhat different. At the time of filming the director and producer donated a sum of money to the school. Prior to the film's release Lopez was offered $45,000, more than his teaching salary, as a fee for his participation in the film's promotional tour; money that Lopez at the time refused. In addition, Lopez, together with all of the children's families saw the film before it went on release and did not complain about the content at the time.

Clearly, this is a fairly controversial and potentially precedent-setting suit, because it challenges industry standards of how documentary film-makers work with their subjects to bring a film together. Generally-speaking documentary subjects are unpaid, but as documentaries grow in popularity with audiences and at the box office it is unsurprising that the "stars" of the movies might desire payment. The ethical question is whether the subject of a documentary is an employee in effect. And if the subject is paid, to what extent this will affect their performance.

Official website for film:
http://chipsquaw.free.fr/etreetavoir/index.html

France's top 5 documentaries of all time

Title	Origin	Distributor	Release date	Gross
Microcosmos	Fr	Bac Films	May 1996	$17m
Etre et Avoir	Fr	Films du Losange	Feb 2002	$8.5m
Winged Migration	Fr	Bac films	Dec 2001	$8m
Bowling for Columbine	Can-US-Ger	Diaphana	Oct 2002	$4.3m
Tous Pres Des Etioles	Fr	Pyramide Dist	March 2001	$458,000

Source: *Screen International*, 21 March 2003, p8

The Unmaking of a Film
Case study on *Lost in La Mancha*
(cert 15) (93mins)

Awards record
European Film awards 2002 – Best Documentary nomination
British Independent awards 2002 – Best Foreign Film (English Language)
Carl Foreman Award for Promising Newcomer, Lucy Darwin (producer), BAFTA 2003 – nomination
Peter Sellers Award for Comedy, Evening Standard British Film Awards 2003 – winner
Best Documentary, Motion Picture Awards 2004 – nomination
Online Film Critics Society 2004 – Best documentary nomination

'There's no shortage of disaster stories in the history of film production, but none have been recorded with such frankness, immediacy and aching sense of disappointment as in Lost in La Mancha... entertaining and instructive... a tantalizing memorial.'
Derek Elley, Variety
Source: www.lostinlamancha.com

Films about Don Quixote have always appeared to have a curse around them. From Sergei Eisenstein in the 1920s to Orson Welles, who died in 1985 whilst making a self-financed film about him, after 15 years on and off in development. Welles's film was completed by Jesus Franco (who served as Welles' second unit director on **Chimes at Midnight**, 1965) and released under the title, **Don Quixote De Orson Welles** (1992).

More recently, in March 1999, Terry Gilliam started pre-production on **The Man Who Killed Don Quixote**, and asked Keith Fulton and Louis Pepe to document it. Little did the two film-makers know where this journey would take them and the heavy ironies that would be played out on screen, with the headstrong, maverick director Gilliam grappling to bring the grandiose fantasist that is the character of Quixote to life. By May 1999, the project was suspended when Gilliam's principle financier withdrew due to insufficient funds. Both films were put on hold, pending Gilliam raising the necessary capital.

By June 2000, the $32 million project was reinstated (unusually using only European finance) and Fulton and Pepe joined forces with producer Lucy Darwin (they had all worked together previously on the documentary **The Hamster Factor and Other Tales of 12 Monkeys**, 1996) to restart their documentary focussing on Gilliam's pre-production process, a process that was hitherto unseen in film. The team were to have unprecedented access to the production and Gilliam agreed to wear a wireless microphone for the duration of the process, to enable them to gain as intimate and 'realistic' portrayal as possible. (Rather remarkably, despite the set-backs and, ultimately disasters that ensued, Gilliam never once turned the microphone off or censored what was said.) Nevertheless, only 6 days into the shoot and due to a whole host of factors (many of them unanticipated and unavoidable): flash floods, camera equipment ruined; funding cuts; studio and location set-backs; scheduling conflicts; the star of the film – Jean Rochefort - becoming ill and a $15million insurance claim (the biggest in European film history), which centred around the insurance company's definition of 'force majeure'; the film production was abandoned and the documentary that Pepe and Fulton had originally set out (or been contracted) to do was not what they ended up with. Their documentary, which is taken from over 80 hours of *vérité* and interview footage, is ultimately about the tragic collapse of a major film production. The finished documentary is an excellent example of the power of hindsight, in that footage which at the time of shooting seemed straightforward, took on much greater resonance

'This film has been so long in the making and so miserable that someone needs to get a film out of it. And it doesn't look like it's going to be me!'
Terry Gilliam
Source:
www.lostinlamancha.com

Super Size Me (2004) is the latest documentary to question the impact of a global business on our lives. Winner of the Directing Prize from the Documentary Jury at the Sundance Film Festival in 2004, the film, which boasts the tagline, A Film of Epic Proportions, *follows 'one artery blocking month' in the life of Director/ Producer Morgan Spurlock during which he eats nothing but McDonalds for breakfast, lunch and dinner. He sets himself only one proviso – that if any of the restaurants ask him if he would like to 'super size' (i.e. get a larger size) then he must submit. Spurlock certainly suffers for his art. He gains a large amount of weight, gets headaches, becomes lethargic, loses his libido but more worryingly, his internal organs are significantly affected. Interestingly, McDonalds refuses to be interviewed by the film-maker and, shortly before it's US release, withdrew the 'super size' option from its menus.*

and poignancy, once the production had collapsed. Gilliam could have pulled the plug on the project, unhappy that the original idea was no longer viable. However, Gilliam remained supportive of the two documentary film-makers work, even joking,

Alongside the fact that the documentary gives a remarkable insight into film production and the process itself, **Lost in La Mancha** makes for an interesting text to study due to the style of the film. Shot on handheld digital video cameras, it also features animation, actual footage from the production, staged readings from the script and Gilliam's original storyboards

Interestingly, the film was released on only 10 prints (i.e. a limited release strategy by Optimum) in the UK but was strategically placed at key independent cinema sites and a few mainstream venues. The film proved to be extremely popular thanks to the excellent media support it had garnered – the on-set drama, together with the offbeat humour, was a draw for audiences. Plus, it made for an excellent insight into the world of film-making, albeit from a negative point of view. Some might say it was required viewing for all would-be film directors / producers as it certainly puts the cliché of the glamorous world of Hollywood and film-making into perspective!

'Audiences want to go and see what is good, whatever it is. It is about entertainment and audiences are definitely responding for that reason.'
Lucy Darwin, producer Lost in La Mancha, *Screen International,* **21 March 2003**

Official website for film:
http://www.lostinlamancha.com/

UK's top 5 documentaries of all time [#]

Title	Origin	Distributor	Release date	Gross
Touching the Void	UK-US	Pathé	2003	£1,681,619*
Bowling For Columbine	Can-Ger-US	Momentum Pictures	2002	£1,667,625
In Bed With Madonna	US	Rank	1991	£1,246,278
Buena Visa Social Club	Ger-UK-US-Fr-Cuba	FilmFour	1999	£955,278
Être et avoir	Fr	Metro-Tartan	2003	£704,582

* still on release at the time of press. Source: AC Nielsen, February 2004
# this chart was compiled in February 2004, prior to the release of *Fahrenheit 9/11*

Afterword

As I was putting the finishing touches to this revision, Michael Moore's 'controversial polemic' (*The Observer*, 23 May 2004), *Fahrenheit 9/11* (2004) became the first feature documentary since *Le Monde du Silence* in 1956 to win the Palme d'Or at the Cannes Film Festival. This is excellent news for Moore, a long time pariah of the film circuit, not least because the award has international status and is highly respected by the industry itself.

One of 18 films in competition at the festival, *Fahrenheit 9/11* received a standing ovation of unprecedented length at its screening, despite the fact that it was considered by many to be the rank outsider. The documentary strongly criticises President George W. Bush's business dealings as well as his jurisdiction over the Iraq war and the American army's torturing of Iraqi prisoners. Ironically when he won the Oscar for *Bowling For Columbine*, Moore was heckled off stage for criticising Bush.

Interestingly, prior to Moore's departure for Cannes he posted an announcement on his website (www.michaelmoore.com) that Disney (the major

Hollywood studio that owns Miramax) had refused to allow producer Miramax to distribute the film, leaving them looking for a new partner. Disney's reticence was attributed to the sensitive nature of the film's content, but Moore and others alleged that the Presidential elections due in autumn 2004 made the studio somewhat wary of releasing a film which is so critical of the incumbent. Disney critics have also pointed out that the release might endanger millions of dollars of tax breaks Disney receives from its Disneyworld complex in Florida as the film may anger the Governor of Florida, Jeb Bush – the President's brother. At the time of writing, however (and no doubt as a partial consequence of Disney's decision), **Fahrenheit 9/11** had subsequently finalised distribution deals in twenty-seven territories – including the UK, where it took £1.3 million in it's first weekend.

* Indeed, Fahrenheit 9/11's opening weekend US box office was in excess of $24m.

The fact that the documentary has garnered such a prestigious award and generated controversy in its wake will mean that **Fahrenheit 9/11** is likely to be seen by even more people theatrically*, and, knowing Moore, he will cover the film's progress in much detail. Moore's **The Big One** (1997) was an account of his publicity tour in support of a book – might we yet see a documentary about a documentary?

Recommended Filmography

The following list of documentaries, most of which received a theatrical release, would be useful when teaching the subject, either for research or to show a class. Particular areas of interest are indicated, as is video and/or Region 2 DVD availability at the time of going to press.

Film	Synopsis	Teaching Interest	Video/DVD
Nanook of the North (Flaherty, 1921, USA)	A portrait of an Eskimo family	The work of early documentary pioneer Robert Flaherty and a point of comparison to *Man of Aran*	**Video** Academy Video (BFI); VHSPal; Cat no: CAV069; Cert: Exempt (E)
Man with a Movie Camera (Vertov, 1929, USSR)	A mosaic of city life (a combination of Kiev, Moscow and Odessa)	Employs advanced cinematic means to produce experimental filmmaking techniques (and the selfreflective camera) which influenced the *cinéma-vérité* movement later; attempts to engage the viewer in a consideration of the relationship between the film and reality; interesting comparison to other city symphonies	**Video** BFI Video; VHSPal; Cat no: BFIV038; Cert: E **DVD** BFI Video; Cat no: BFIVD502; Cert: E (extras include: choice of three soundtracks, filmmakers' biographies and poster images)
Man of Aran (Flaherty, 1934, GB)	The life of a crofting and fishing community in Ireland	Compare with Flaherty's *Nanook of the North*; early documentary filmmaking technique	**Video** Video Collection Int.; VHSPal; Cat no: VC3472; Cert: U
New Deal Documentaries (Lorentz, Ivens, McClure, 1934-40, USA)	A unique collection of films produced by the US Federal Government in the 'New Deal' era. Contains *The Plow that Broke the Plains, The River, The Power and the Land* and *The New Frontier*	Depictions of a tragic chapter in American history that use an affecting combination of stirring visual imagery and poetic narration	**Video** Connoisseur Video (BFI); VHSPal; Cat no: CAV067; Cert: E

Fires were Started (Jennings, 1943, GB)	Twenty-four hours in the life of a National Fire Service unit during the Second World War	Intended as a training film and then released theatrically as propaganda; focuses on an institution; compare to similar, more current documentaries such as 999; use of reenactment as a legitimate documentary technique	N/A
Don't Look Back (Pennebaker, 1967, USA)	Portrait of Bob Dylan's tour of 1965	Use of hand-held camera technique; early direct cinema feature; representation of a pop icon and an attempt to capture an era	**DVD** Cat no: EREDV327; Cert: E
The Sorrow and the Pity (Ophuls, 1970, Fr/Switz/Ger)	Portrait of France during the German Occupation in the Second World War	Ambitious 4 1/2 hr film which is nevertheless very powerful; the bulk of the footage is interviews with those who lived through the Nazi threat and what has been said is then immediately annotated; interesting oral history and essay	**DVD** due for release autumn 2004
Pumping Iron (Butler, 1976, USA)	The Mr Olympia competition in America	Adapted from a book of the same name; it has the first appearance of Arnold Schwarzeneggar; interesting representation of men and masculinity; compare to the sequel - *Pumping Iron II: The Women*	**DVD** Warner Home Video; Cat no: D025251; Cert: PG
Best Boy (Wohl, 1976, USA)	The life of a mentally handicapped 33 year old man whose parents are elderly and frail	Representation of age and disability; film as a tool for provoking emotion	**Video** Academy Video (BFI); VHSPal; Cat no: CAV032; Cert: E

The Day After Trinity (Else, 1980, USA)	Account of Los Alamos in 1941 where the first atomic bomb was created to try to bring the Second World War to an end	Uses real footage of the bomb and anecdotal evidence; representation of war; attempt at a moral subtext	N/A
The Atomic Café (K. Rafferty, Loader and P. Rafferty, 1982, USA)	A compilation of excerpts from the 40s and 50s which looks at the American Government's use of the nuclear bomb	Use of archive footage; attempts (and fails...) to use humour in the editing; provides no social context for the use of the bomb; interesting comparison to *The Day After Trinity*	**Video** Academy Video (BFI); VHSPal; Cat no: CAV031; Cert: 12
Shoah (Lanzmann, 1985, Fr)	Highly acclaimed nine hour meditation on the Holocaust	Uses testimonies and re-enactment but no historical footage to explore the issue; interesting from a 'realism' perspective	N/A
The Thin Blue Line (Morris, 1988, USA)	Explores the case of a man found guilty of murdering a Dallas policeman in 1976 and questions his guilt	Attempts to disprove a judicial decision and uncover 'the truth'; compare to current examples of television investigative journalism – *The Cook Report*; *MacIntyre Undercover*	**Video** BFI; VHS Pal; Cat no: BFIV085; Cert: 15
For All Mankind (Reinhert, 1989, USA)	Depiction of an Apollo moon flight	Comprises footage taken from NASA records edited to create one seamless journey; end credit says filmed 'on location'!	N/A
Roger and Me (Moore, 1989, USA)	Exploration of the closure of a General Motors factory and the impact on a community	Use of humour and irony; representation of blue-collar workers and the unemployed; it caused controversy and was accused of inaccuracy and contrivance in order to prove a point	**DVD** Warner Home Video; Cat no: D027645; Cert: 15

Hearts of Darkness: A Filmmaker's Apocalypse (Bahr & Hickenlooper, 1991, USA)	The making of *Apocalypse Now* in 1976	Behind-the-scenes footage, with interesting use of anecdote and inside account of filmmaking	N/A
Hoop Dreams (James, 1994, USA)	Two black teenagers pursue their dream of playing basketball professionally	Representation of race, class and the American Dream; use of a linear narrative structure which is usually employed within fiction films	**Video** Cinema Club; VHSPal; Cat no: CC8416; Cert E
When We Were Kings (Gast, 1996, USA)	Depicts the famous 'Rumble in the Jungle' fight for the heavyweight championship between Muhammed Ali and George Foreman in 1974 and features the flamboyant promoter Don King	Released 22 years after the event; the film was originally intended to focus on the concert which accompanied the fight and starred BB King and James Brown, but due to copyright and funding problems the footage was reedited to focus on the fight itself	**Video** Universal Pictures Video; VHSPal; Cat no: 0783563; Cert: PG **DVD** Universal Pictures DVD; Cat no: 9025712; Cert: PG
Kurt and Courtney (Broomfield, 1998, USA)	A portrait of the lead singer of rock band Nirvana, Kurt Cobain, and his suicide	Cobain's wife Courtney Love infamously refused to co-operate with the |film or allow his |music to be played; Broomfield's interview technique makes him very much a part of the film - indeed his film-in-the-making arguably becomes the subject of the film	**DVD** Optimum Home Entertainment; Cat no: OPTD0023; Cert: 15

The Last Days (Moll, 1998, USA)	Five Jewish Hungarians, now U.S. citizens, tell of their experiences during the Second World War	The interviews are recorded in the subjects' homes and achieved using 35mm, widescreen tripod-shot which is then interspersed with slow-motion archive footage, underpinned with a powerful musical score. Interesting comparison to *Shoah*	N/A
Buena Vista Social Club (Wenders, 1998, Ger)	A group of legendary Cuban musicians (some as old as 90) are brought together to record a CD produced by Ry Cooder	Incorporates footage from the recording through to the actual concerts, as well as individual interviews with the musicians	**Video** Cinema Club; VHSPal; Cat no: CC9518; Cert: E **DVD** Cinema Club; Cat no: CCD9519; Cert: E
One Day in September (MacDonald, 1999, UK)	The story of the 1972 Munich Olympics, where Palestinian athletes were murdered by Israeli terrorists	Uses a blend of archive footage and interview (including one with the sole surviving terrorist); use of cliched shots at the beginning lulls the audience before unveiling a succession of tragic facts as well as talking head interviews, found footage and reenactment. Compare to Leni Riefenstahl's *Olympia* (1938) and Kon Ichikawa's *Tokyo Olympiad 1964* (1965)	**Video** Redbus; VHSPal; Cat no. S093125; Cert: 15
Dogtown and Z Boys Dir. Stacy Peralta (2001)	Focus on the transformation of skateboarding from its former image as a land-bound pastime for surfers to its status today as an extreme and acrobatic sport in its own right.	Useful for representation and a consideration of popular culture / youth culture.	**DVD** Columbia Tri-Star; Cat no: CDR33377; Cert: 15

Scratch Dir. Doug Pray (2001)	Feature-length documentary about hip-hop DJing, otherwise known as turntablism, from the South Bronx in the 1970s to present-day San Francisco.	Useful for representation and a consideration of popular culture.	**DVD** Momentum; Cat no: MP228D; Cert: 15
Spellbound Dir. Jeffrey Blitz (2002)	Eight US youngsters on their quest to win the 1999 National Spelling Bee.	Good source for issues around character and representation.	**Video** Metrodome; VHSPal; Cat no. MTS8071; Cert: U **DVD** Metrodome: Cat no: MTD5137; Cert: U (extras include deleted scenes)
Bowling for Columbine Dir. Michael Moore (2002)	Academy Award winning exploration of America's predilection for gun violence.	Good stimulus material for issues of ideology, hegemony and notions of bias / audience positioning. A key example of Moore's work, useful to compare his style to Broomfield's	**Video** Momentum; VHSPal; Cat no: MP235V; Cert: 15 **DVD** Momentum; Cat no: MP235D; Cert: 15
Lost in La Mancha Dir. Keith Fulton & Louis Pepe (2002)	Captures Terry Gilliam's attempt to get his film *The Man Who Killed Don Quixote* off the ground.	Interesting for focusing on the 'warts and all' behind the scenes story of a film production.	**Video** Optimum; VHSPal; Cat no: OPTV0022; Cert: 15 **DVD** Optimum; Cat no: OPTD0022; Cert 15 (extras include interviews with principals and storyboards)
Être et Avoir Dir. Nicolas Philibert (2002)	Portrait of a one-room school in rural France, where the students (ranging in age from 4 to 11) are educated by a single dedicated teacher.	Useful for a consideration of institution and representation as well as the issue of intellectual property that arose around the filming.	**Video** Tartan; VHSPal; Cat no: TVT1387; Cert: U **DVD** Tartan: Cat no: TVD3450; Cert U

The Kid Stays in the Picture Dir. Nanette Burstein & Brett Morgen (2002)	Focus on legendary Paramount producer and studio chief Robert Evans, the first actor ever to run a film studio.	Useful for a consideration of institution, representation and use of archive footage.	**Video** Momentum; VHSPal; Cat no: MP242V; Cert 15 **DVD** Momentum; Cat no: MP242D; Cert: 15
Standing in the Shadows of Motown Dir. Paul Justman (2002)	Documentary about the Funk Brothers, a group of Detroit musicians who backed up dozens of Motown artists, with the use of archival footage, still photos, narration, interviews, re-creation scenes, 20 Motown master tracks, and twelve new live performances of Motown classics with the Brothers backing up contemporary performers.	An excellent example of music documentary.	**DVD** Momentum; Cat no: MP259D; Cert: PG
Aileen Wournos: Life and Death of a Serial Killer Dir. Nick Broomfield & Joan Churchill (2003)	Broomfield's follow-up documentary on Wuornos, a highway prostitute who was executed in 2002 for killing seven men in the state of Florida. This second instalment includes the film-maker's testimony at Wournos's appeal.	Useful for a consideration of Broomfield's work, issues of representation and ideology as well as the use of Broomfield's original documentary within Wournos's appeal. Students could also consider the film in terms of its anti-death penalty stance and the fact that it raises questions about executing the mentally ill.	**DVD** Optimum; Cat no: OPTD0058; Cert 15

The Fog of War Dir. Erroll Morris (2003)	Academy Award-winning documentary about Robert McNamara, Secretary of Defence in the Kennedy and Johnson administrations, who subsequently became President of the World Bank. The documentary combines an interview with McNamara discussing some of the tragedies and glories of the 20th Century, archival footage, documents, and an original score by Philip Glass.	Good stimulus material for issues of ideology, hegemony, the nature and representation of modern war and notions of bias / audience positioning.	**DVD** Columbia Tri-Star Home Video; Cat no: CDR35046; Cert: PG (released autumn 2004)
Touching the Void Dir. Kevin MacDonald (2003)	BAFTA award winning true story of two climbers and their perilous journey up the west face of Siula Grande in the Peruvian Andes in 1985.	Useful for use of recreation of key scenes/ docudrama, use of interviews and special effects.	**Video** Video Collection; VHSPal; Cat no: VC3974; Cert: 15 **DVD** VCD0373; Cat no: VCD0373; Cert 15
Super Size Me Dir. Morgan Spurlock (2004)	An irreverent look at obesity in America and one of its main sources - fast food corporations. The film-maker eats nothing but McDonalds meals for 30 days, three times a day, in a bid to explore the physical and mental effects such a diet has on the human body. The film won Best Director award at Sundance Festival (2004)	Useful for point of view, institution and ideology.	N/A at time of writing but likely to be available by early 2005

Recommended Further Reading

Aitken, Ian, *The Documentary Film Movement*, Edinburgh: Edinburgh University Press, 1998.

Barnouw, Erik, *A History of the Non- Fiction Film*, 3rd edn., New York: Oxford University Press, 1993.

Barsam, Richard Meran (ed.), *Non-Fiction Film Theory and Criticism*, New York: Dutton, 1976.

Barsam, Richard Meran, *Non-Fiction Films: A Critical History*, Bloomington: Indiana University Press, 1992,

Barsam, Richard Meran, *The Vision of Robert Flaherty: The Artist as Myth and Film-Maker*, Bloomington: Indiana University Press, 1988.

Bernard, Sheila Curran, *Documentary Storytelling*, Oxford: Focal Press, 2003.

Bruzzi, Stella, *New Documentary*, London: Routledge, 2000.

Corner, John (ed.), *Documentary and the Mass Media*, London: Edward Arnold, 1986.

Corner, John, *The Art of Record: A Critical Introduction to Documentary*, Manchester: Manchester University Press, 1996.

Hardy, Forsyth, *John Grierson: A Documentary Biography*, London: Faber and Faber, 1979.

Hight, Craig, *Faking It*, Manchester: Manchester University Press, 2001.

Kriwaczeck, Paul, *Documentary for the Small Screen*, Oxford: Focal Press, 1997.

Levin, G. Roy, *Documentary Explorations: Fifteen Interviews with Film- Makers*, Garden City, NY: Doubleday, 1971.

Lewis, Jacob, *The Documentary Tradition: From Nanook to Woodstock*, New York: W W Norton, 1971.

MacDonald, Kevin and Cousins, Mark, *Imagining Reality: The Faber Book of Documentary*, London: Faber, 1998.

Nichols, Bill, *Documentary Theory and Practice*, Screen vol. 17 no.4, Winter 1976/77.

Nichols, Bill, *Representing Reality*, Bloomington: Indiana University Press, 1991.

Nichols, Bill, *Introduction to Documentary*, Indiana: Indiana University Press, 2001.

Renov, Michael (ed.), *Theorizing Documentary*, New York: Routledge, 1993.

Renov, Michael, *The Subject of Documentary*, Minnesota: University of Minnesota Press, 2004.

Rabiger, Michael, *Directing the Documentary*, 4th edn, Boston: Focal Press, 2004.

Rosenthal, Alan, *The New Documentary in Action*, Los Angeles: University of California Press, 1972.

Rosenthal, Alan, *The Documentary Conscience: A Casebook in Film-making*, Berkeley: University of California Press, 1980.

Rosenthal, Alan, *Writing, Directing and Producing Documentary Films*, Carbondale, IL: Southern Illinois University Press, 1990.

Rotha, Paul, *Documentary Film*, New York: Hastings House, 1952.

Rothman, William, *Documentary Film Classics*, Cambridge: Cambridge University Press, 1997.

Sussex, E., *The Rise and Fall of British Documentary*, Los Angeles: University of California Press, 1972.

Williams, Christopher (ed.), *Realism in the Cinema*, London: BFI, 1980.

Winston, Brian, *Claiming the Real*, London: BFI, 1995.

Websites of Interest

www.sidf.co.uk - Sheffield International Documentary Film Festival. An annual event, usually held around October.

www.docos.com - US documentary information site, very much industry focused. Free daily e-mail newsletter available.

http://www.realityfilm.com/study/index.html useful site which gives good resources, definitions and reviews.

www.edfilmfest.org.uk - Edinburgh International Film Festival, which has a documentary section in the programme. Runs annually in August.

www.bfi.org.uk - British Film Institute site that includes full listing of titles available from BFI Video.

www.documentaryfilms.net – good site for films reviews, info on documentary festivals, production companies, resources, etc.

www.docfilm.weblogsinc.com – info on the latest documentary releases, issues and industry news.

www.hotdocs.ca – Hot Docs Canadian International Documentary Festival is North America's largest documentary festival; this website gives info on the festival and its programme.

www.filmsite.org/docfilms.html – interesting essay on the documentary genre.

www.nd.edu/~jgodmilo/reality – interesting abstract of conversation between Jill Godmilow and Ann-Louise Shapiro which considers the concept of realism in documentary.

www.documentary.org – website for the International Documentary Association – contains resource info, reviews, industry news, etc.

www.worldfilm.about.com/od/ documentaryfilms – contains comprehensive access to articles and resources on documentary feature films.

www.imdb.com - Internet Movie Database.

www.bbc.co.uk - BBC Online, ideal starting point for research.

www.tes.co.uk - *The Times Education Supplement*.

www.guardian.co.uk - The *Guardian* and *Observer* newspapers.

www.independent.co.uk - The *Independent* newspaper.

www.telegraph.co.uk - The *Telegraph* newspaper.